TALKING DRUMS OF AFRICA

To My Father and Mother

TALKING DRUMS OF AFRICA

by

J. F. CARRINGTON, B.Sc., Ph.D.

The Baptist Missionary Society, Yakusu
Near Stanleyville, Belgian Congo

NEGRO UNIVERSITIES PRESS
NEW YORK

The Library of Congress cataloged this book as follows:

Carrington, John F
    Talking drums of Africa, by J. F. Carrington. New
York, Negro Universities Press ₍1969₎

    96 p. Illus. 23 cm.

    Reprint of the 1949 ed.
    Bibliography : p. 91–93.

    1. Drum language. 2. Musical instruments, African. 3. Musical
instruments, Primitive. 4. Signals and signaling. I. Title.

ML1035.C3 1969	789′.1	70–77195
SBN 8371-1292-3		MARC
Library of Congress	69 ₍3₎	MN

Originally published in 1949 by The Carey Kingsgate Press,
London.

Reprinted in 1969 by Negro University Press, Greenwood Press.

A division of Congressional Information Service, Inc.
88 Post Road West, Westport, Connecticut 06881

Library of Congress catalog card number 70-77195
ISBN 0-8371-1292-3

Printed in the United States of America

10 9 8 7 6 5 4

CONTENTS

5

ILLUSTRATIONS

CHAPTER I

INTRODUCTION

DURING my first few months as a missionary of the Baptist
Missionary Society in the Stanleyville area of Belgian Congo, I
was sent out, along with a more experienced colleague, to the
villages of the Bambɔlε forest on the south bank of the Congo.
We had been working for some days in a village called Yawiʃa
and we planned to make a half-day trip to the neighbouring town
of Yaongama, some seven or eight miles away. When we arrived
at Yaongama I was surprised to find the village teacher, the
medical assistant and the church members all awaiting us in their
schoolroom. Without attempting to discover by what means the
news of our approach had reached the villagers (we had sent no
messenger from Yawiʃa) we got down to the work for the day.
But my silent queries were answered during an address by the
native pastor which wound up our business at the village. He
put a question to the assembled congregation in order to bring
home some point in his talk.

'How did we know the white men were coming to-day?' he
asked.

'By the drum message,' came the reply.

On making inquiries after the meeting, I found that soon after
our departure from Yawiʃa the villagers there had sent a message
by the drum to Yaongama informing the church members to
be ready to meet the B.M.S. white men who were on their
way.

Stories of this kind are common in travel books about Africa.
In a book edited by Knox and entitled *Travels into the Inland
parts of Africa*, there is a description of a journey to villages of the
Mandingo country of West Africa by Francis Moore who left
England in 1730. He writes:

> In almost every town they have a kind of drum of a very
> large size called a tangtang which they only beat at the
> approach of an enemy or on some very extraordinary
> occasion to call the inhabitants of the neighbouring towns to
> their assistance. . . .

A century later, in *A Narrative of the Expedition sent by Her Majesty's Government to the River Niger in 1841*, a similar story is told. Referring to a native named Glasgow, the writers say:

> He also said that they could communicate by this means at very great distance by the war drum which is kept in every village to give and repeat these signals; so that there is intimation of danger long before the enemy can attack them. We are often surprised to find the sound of the trumpet so well understood in our military evolutions, but how far short that falls of the result arrived at by these untutored savages. This method of communication is no doubt employed by slave dealers to give notice of the movements of our cruisers.

This extract is interesting in showing the distinction between drum signalling and drum talking. The former is common in most countries of the world, being especially used in military operations. Our well-known bugle calls are examples of the same kind of signals although a different instrument is used to send them. But the drum signals described by Glasgow are of a different kind; they have a language basis and can be modified to beat out messages which cover almost any situation arising in native life.

On his epoch-making journey across Africa from 1875 to 1877, H. M. Stanley passed through the drum language area of the continent. He mentions again and again the 'sonorous war-drums' and suspects that they are used to stimulate the natives to attack him and his fellow-travellers. In a later book which describes his experiences in the Congo when he returned there to organize the *État Indépendant du Congo* on behalf of King Leopold II of the Belgians, Stanley gives an account of these remarkable drums. Speaking of the baEna tribe living on the banks of the Congo at the cataracts which are now called Stanley Falls he says:

> The islanders have not yet adopted electric signals but possess, however, a system of communication quite as effective. Their huge drums by being struck in different parts convey language as clear to the initiated as vocal speech. . . .

The baEna tribes still possess and use such talking drums. They are not the same as those which Stanley saw, for the life of a talking drum in Central Africa does not exceed forty or fifty years, but they are like them and used in just the same way.

The following quotation, from R. E. Dennett (3. p. 76) illustrates the use of the drum for relaying messages from village to village until the news is carried for quite a considerable distance. He is describing the drums of the Loango area, north of the mouth of the Congo river.

> In 1881 we in Landana heard of the wreck of the mail steamer, *Ethiopia*, sixty or seventy miles away one or two hours after its actual occurrence in Luango, by drum message . . . a good operator with his drumsticks can say anything he likes upon it (the drum) in his dialect . . . The drum language, so-called, is not limited to a few sentences but, given a good operator, and a good listener, comprehends all a man can say.

The value of this method of communication in a country where road travel is often impossible and river travel is tedious was quickly recognized by early colonists. As early as 1899 (and even before that date) Belgian Government officers in the Congo were quick to use the drum for communicating orders to native chiefs under them. A. B. Lloyd (5. p. 353) tells of the signalling drum of the tribes along the banks of the Aruwimi river (these people are the bAngwa whose present-day method of drumming is referred to later) (cf. p. 51). He says:

> I was told that from one village to another, a distance of over a hundred miles, a message could be sent in less than two hours and I quite believe it possible to be done in much less time. The Belgian officers use this method of communication with the natives, always keeping a drum on the station and a man that can beat it.

One of the most ingenious uses of the talking drum as an aid to colonization must surely be that described by Lieutenant Gilmont in 1877, concerning an officer of the *État Indépendant du Congo*.

> An officer commissioned with the task of quelling a revolt among the natives (for there are revolts in all countries of the world) had some knowledge of the telegraphic language used

by the indigenous peoples. One evening he took, by surprise, a large talking drum and beat out again and again:

luiza quo, luiza quo . . . come here, come here.

The natives, believing the white man to be some distance away, presented themselves full of confidence and were roped in one by one as they came. Thus it was that all hostilities were terminated peacefully.[1]

Doubt has been cast on the veracity of stories such as these, however. Fairly recently the question of drum languages was raised in a B.B.C. discussion and the answers given showed that only the vaguest of information was to hand.[2] In a book published a short time ago[3] telepathic communication was put forward as a means by which the drums could broadcast their messages. It is certainly true that some accounts of the drum languages of Africa have been seriously exaggerated. As A. J. H. Goodwin says:

> The drum language of West Africa has been built up by careless journalism into one of the wonders of the world. Messages sent by this means have been described as covering great areas at speeds sometimes faster than that of sound. . . . (1. p. 233).

Yet the actual mechanism of message transmission by drums and other instruments has been worked out by a number of ethnologists and linguists during the past fifty years. Their researches extend over a wide area in West and Central Africa. The results, however, are only available in scientific journals not easily procurable and the greater part are in languages other than English (the most important are listed in an appendix to this book). It is the object of this account of the drum languages of Africa to present the findings of such investigators together with my own experience of drum talking in the Stanleyville area of Belgian Congo — an area not referred to by other workers. Thus I hope to make it clear that there is no doubt about the possibility of 'talking' on the drum, that messages are sent regularly in many parts of Africa and that there is no mystery whatever in the method used by many skilled Africans to pass on news to their neighbours.

---

[1] Quoted in VAN OVERBERGH, *Les Mayombe*, Brussels 1907.
[2] cf. the letter, 'News by drum beats', *Radio Times*, June 9th, 1944.
[3] R. St. BARBE BAKER, *Africa Drums*, London 1942.

CHAPTER II

CENTRAL AFRICAN LANGUAGES AND OUR OWN [1]

SINCE the 'talking' of an African drum is essentially a question of language and not of conventional signals like the bugle calls of European armies, we can only hope to understand the nature of the messages sent when we have grasped the essential features of the spoken tongues of Africa. We can say with confidence that, had early explorers been more familiar with the nature of the languages used by African peoples, there would never have been any mystery about the talking drums.

There is an immense variety of languages in Africa. This is partly due to the lack of easy communications in a country of forest and swamp, rivers, mountains and deserts; partly to the absence of dominating tribes over large areas (until comparatively recent years, when Arabic and European civilizations began to spread over the continent); and partly to the character of many African communities which prefer to live in small, isolated 'stateless societies', self-sufficient and owing allegiance to no other group. These reasons are, of course, interdependent, but they have been responsible for the development of innumerable languages and dialect forms only some of which have hitherto been reduced to writing or studied by 'foreigners'. So it is, for instance, that in the boys' school at Yakusu there are representatives of nine different tribes each with its own tongue (one of these being chosen as the medium of instruction). Estimates of the total number of languages to be found in Africa depend a great deal on what is considered to be a language and what is regarded as a dialect form of a language. A recent estimate for one group of African tongues — the Bantu family (see later) — giving one hundred and fifty [2] as the number of 'dialects' is very conservative. But that figure will serve to show how complicated is the task of getting to know the structure and characteristic features of the language families of Africa.

[1] Readers not interested in language study are advised to skip this chapter, although it contains the key to the 'secret' of the drum language as explained in chapter IV.
[2] BODMER, F., *The Loom of Language*, London 1941, p. 209.

Where a powerful tribe has been able to extend its influence by conquest or commerce, there a single language becomes known over a comparatively wide area. This is true of the Kongo language in the western section of Belgian Congo. When Diego

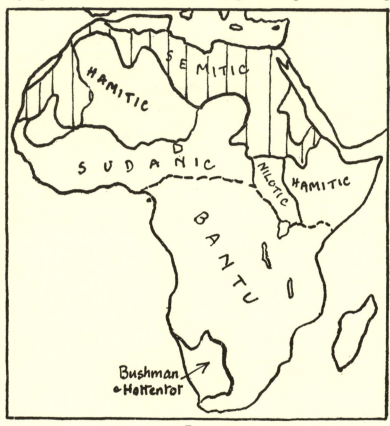

FIG. 1

Map showing the language groups of Africa

Cão visited the mouth of the Congo river in 1482 he heard of the King of Kongo and his kingdom, already in existence at that early date. To a much less degree, the Kele language has become known over an area wider than that occupied by the Lokele tribe because this people is a riverine group, given to trading up and down the river in canoes. Their language has thus become the 'market-language' of the Stanleyville area.

To-day, with easier communications as a result of the white man's entry into Africa and as a result of Arabic influence from the east and the north, some languages are becoming known over very wide areas and serve as 'trade' languages, or *linguae francae*. Thus Swahili and its dialect forms serve to carry the traveller from the east coast of Africa right over to the lake region and beyond into Belgian Congo. Where Swahili is no longer understood (the language 'water-shed' is to be found in the Yakusu area) another widely known language, Ngala, will serve to take the traveller down to Stanley Pool and almost to the west coast.

But in our attempt to seek an understanding of the African talking drum we shall not concern ourselves with these widely known trade languages. For the language used on the drum is the local language of the small tribal group. Even where a trade language such as Ngala is known and used, the members of the tribal group will still use their own tongue for intercommunication; this tribal language is still the language learned by a child at its mother's knee and it forms the basis of the drum language.

THE GROUPS OF AFRICAN LANGUAGES

Thanks to the researches of missionaries, explorers and Government officers, we are in possession to-day of a fair amount of information about African languages from many different parts of the continent. This information is sufficient to enable us to classify the languages spoken in Africa into a few main groups and to subdivide these main groups into numerous language clusters and families. The main groups recognized are:

Bushman languages
Negro languages, divided into:
    Sudanic languages
    Nilotic languages and
    Bantu languages
Hamito-Semitic languages.

The accompanying map shows how these languages are distributed over Africa.

The names given to the main language groups are for the most part self-explanatory. But the name 'bantu' may need some clarification, especially as this group, together with the Sudanic group, provides the majority, if not all, of the drum languages which form the subject of our study in this book. Early students of the languages spoken by Africans in West, East, South and Central Africa found there was a striking resemblance in some corresponding words in the various tongues. The following Table of words taken from representative Bantu languages shows this resemblance.

TABLE I

Of corresponding words in different Bantu languages
Note that singular and plural forms are given for the nouns. The adjectival forms are written as if they refer to a man. The language Mbane is NOT bantu, but probably Sudanic. It is included as a 'control' to show that the characteristics found in the bantu group are not reproduced in the Sudanic family

English	Swahili (East Africa)	Zulu (south)	Kongo (west)	Kele (centre)	Nkundo (centre)	Mbane (north-centre)
eye sing. plur.	jico maco	iso	disu mesu	liso baiso	liso baiso	lale lase
tongue	ulimi ndimi	ulimi	ludimi tudimi	lolamɛ ndamɛ	lolemi ndemi	mine mise
man (homo)	mtu watu	umuntu	muntu bantu	boto bato	bonto banto	njwa njwe
one	mmoja	—	moci	ɔmɔi	ɔmɔ	gima
evil	mbaya	–bi	ambi	bobe	bobe	sisige

Clearly there is a resemblance among all the Bantu words with a given meaning. The word for 'man' is typical of the rest; its 'root', that is, the part of the word which does not change to give singular and plural forms, is -tu or something very like -tu such as -to, -nto, -ntu, etc. This resemblance of form for the word 'man' was early recognized and gave the name to the whole group of languages — they were called the 'bantu' languages.

It will be realized from the table above that the form of the word for 'man' is not the only criterion determining whether a language shall fall into the 'bantu' or into another group. Many other roots are very similar in different languages of the bantu family. Meinhof has published a list of over five hundred roots which are shown to occur in many different bantu tongues and which, together, form what he calls Ur-Bantu; that is, a kind of parent form of the many bantu dialects extant to-day.

Grammatical structure also shows similarities. Notice in the table how the bantu languages given form plural and singular by changing a small part of the word (a prefix) in front of the root. On the other hand Mbane, which is not bantu, makes plural and singular forms by changing suffixes, a method of plural formation which is more like that often used in English and French.

LEARNING AN AFRICAN LANGUAGE

Anyone who has tried to learn a language different from his own soon realizes that he must accustom his voice to different sounds and different ways of making such sounds from those occurring in his own tongue. These differences in language construction are of different kinds. First of all there are differences in the vowels and consonants which make up the new language. An Englishman learning French must practise carefully the sound of *u* in *une* or the nasal vowel of the word *pont*, for the exact equivalents of these sounds are not to be found in his mother tongue. The difficulty of the German in learning to pronounce *th* in *the* and *that* is proverbial, while Welshmen tell us that English tongues are not long enough to be able to pronounce some of the consonants peculiar to the Welsh language. Similarly, in learning to speak an African language there are new sounds to acquire. The 'click-consonants' of some South African languages are extreme examples of these new sounds. They do not occur in normal European speech although most people have used at least two of them in addressing horses and cows and in expressions of annoyance (tut-tut)! In African languages there often occur sounds which must be represented by new signs not found in European printing and writing. These new signs are explained, in so far as they find their way into this book, in the accompanying appendix. Sometimes a European, struggling with the pronunciation of an obscure sound in an African tongue, cannot refrain from asking himself whether thick lips and filed teeth are not, after all, necessary for acquiring a real 'native' accent!

Secondly, there are differences of *stress* between the new language to be learned and the one already known. That stress is an important feature of a European language can readily be inferred from a few English examples. Thus the word *compress* can have two meanings according to the stress imparted to the component syllables. Spoken with the stress on the second syllable, *com*PRESS, the word is a verb and has to do with squeezing. But as COM*press*, it is a noun representing something usually put on hot at inflamed points in the body. Similarly with words such as *collect, compact, progress* and so on. This special feature of stress differs in different languages. Corresponding words in French, Dutch, German and English may have very similar spelling and even vowel pronunciation, but they often show great differences in the stress values given to the component syllables. So, too, in African languages, there are definite stress patterns which must be learned by the student who wishes to acquire a reasonably good 'accent'. Many Europeans tend to carry over into the native African language the stress patterns of their own mother tongue, with the result that their manner of speaking is sometimes unintelligible to the Africans who are addressed by them. The stress patterns of a word are important to the drummer using that word in his drum message, for the drummed word must imitate the stress value of the syllables.

A third kind of difference between languages of different peoples is that known as 'tone' or 'musical intonation'. We are now dealing with a difference which is of vital importance to any discussion on the nature of the drum languages. Musical intonation is a feature of European as well as African languages. In English we are able to distinguish meaning by using the same words with a different intonation. Take, for instance, the one sentence: *he went outside*. We can give this sentence six different meanings according to the intonation of the syllables of which it is composed. Thus (*see the appendix for the point notation*):

he went outside [. . . .] an account of what he did
he went outside [˙ . . .] not his wife, but *he* went outside
he went outside [. . . ⟍] in answer to a question as to where
  he went
he went outside [. . ˙ .] not inside but *out*side
he went outside [. . . ╱] did he go outside, really?
he went outside [˙ ˙ ˙ ╱] 'garn with yer!' . . . I don't believe
  he went outside

and so on. Differences of stress are also playing a part in making these meaning differences, but tone or musical pitch of the syllables is more important. Once again, the patterns of one language are not necessarily those of another. How many English students of French are guilty of speaking correct French vowels and consonants with an English intonation and thereby betraying to a Frenchman their foreign origin? It is only when a foreigner deliberately sets out to acquire the correct tonal patterns of a language in addition to correct sound-patterns and stress that he can hope to get rid of a foreign accent.

When we come to the study of African languages we find that in very many cases the musical pattern or tone of the language plays a very important part in distinguishing meaning. First of all there is the kind of tone-pattern we have just noted for English and other European tongues, where the general tone pattern of the sentence serves to differentiate a question from a statement of fact or to make an emphasis on one word of the sentence. The former is especially important in African languages because it may be the only way of asking a question without the use of special interrogative words. Here are two examples from Kele and Ngwana (a dialect form of Swahili):

English	tone	Kele	tone
he has really come	[. . ˙ ˙ .]	asooya wewe	[. ˙ . ˙ \ .]
has he really come?	[˙ ˙ ⁄ ˙ ˙]	asooya wewe?	[. ˙ . ˙ \ ˙]

English	tone	Ngwana	tone
he has really come	[. . ˙ ˙ .]	amekuya kweli	[. . ˙ . ˙ .]
has he really come?	[˙ ˙ ⁄ ˙ ˙]	amekuya kweli?	[. . ˙ . ˙ ˙]

Notice that in the African languages the general tone pattern is kept high for the question but is allowed to fall gradually throughout the sentence and markedly at the end for the statement of fact.

But there is a more important aspect of tone in Bantu languages like Kele and Sudanic languages like Mbane. Because this aspect does not occur in English, French, German, Dutch and other similar languages it was overlooked for a long time by early workers on African tongues.[1] It is this aspect of tone which lies at the root of all drum languages and gives the explanation of the

---

[1] Exception must be made here, however, of the work of the Baptist missionary, John Whitehead, whose Bobangi Grammar, published in 1893, gives a detailed, accurate account of tones.

mechanism of the drum messages. We may state briefly the principle of the tonal nature of such African languages in the following words:

> each syllable of a language such as Kele or Mbane possesses a fixed tone which is fundamentally high or low and which must be maintained wherever this syllable occurs in a sentence unless modified according to certain clearly defined and regular tonal rules.

The examples we have already given will serve to illustrate this principle. Compare first of all the English statement of fact with the question: *Has he really come?* The word *he* has distinct tones; in the former case it is low in tone while in the latter case it is high. Similarly for the word *has*. The tones of *really* are also different; the statement of fact gives two high tones to the syllables of this word, but the question shows a low tone followed by a high tone so as to produce a glide from low to high. So that in English, tones of similar syllables can obviously change, the change depending on the kind of work which the words containing the syllables have to do (to state a fact or to ask a question, for instance). But in an African language like Kele this never occurs. Examine the word *asooya* in the two sentences. In both cases the syllables have the same tonal pattern, namely: low, high, low high. The Ngwana word *amekuya* is also the same in both sentences: low, low, high, low. And these tonal patterns for *asooya* or *amekuya* must be maintained the same wherever the words occur. Pick out the tones of the former in this Kele sentence: they are clearly the same as before.

[· ·   .. . · .   .. .   .. ·   , · . . .. ·..·]
sango waɛ asooya kwani la asoonga mbo etungani yaɛ asooya
[· ·   . . .]
amamwito lande

your father has come now and he says that your younger brother has come with him

The actual pitch given to the component syllables is not of great importance. Clearly, a child will give a pitch to his syllables, whether high or low, the physical frequency of which is much greater than the pitches of syllables spoken by an adult. Moreover, the actual *difference* in pitch between high and low tones is not of any great importance, different individuals and different village groups often varying considerably in this respect. When I was struggling to acquire a correct tonal pattern to my own attempts at speaking Kele an old native workman told me I was speaking Kele like a forest man would speak it, and pointed out that I went 'up and down too much'. What is important, however, is that a difference in pitch shall be maintained between high- and low-toned syllables. If a foreigner says the word *asooya* with tones [. . ˙ .] or [. ˙ ˙ .] or [. . . .] etc., then he is speaking Kele with a foreign accent and a native will not easily grasp what he has to say.

Unfortunately, speaking a language like Kele or Mbane with wrong tonal patterns does not only lead to a foreign accent and hence difficulty of comprehension on the part of the listener — it may lead to serious misunderstanding. For Kele (and the same is true of many other Bantu and Sudanic tongues) has a number of words which are alike in sound-patterns and in stress and hence are written alike in our European books, but they differ in meaning according to their tonal patterns. Thus:

(1) *luwaka*   [. ˙ ˙]   fish!   (imperative of the verb)
    luwaka   [˙ ˙ ˙]   know!   (idem   )

(2) *lukaka*   [. ˙ ˙]   seek!   (idem   )
    lukaka   [˙ ˙ ˙]   paddle! (idem   )

(3) *ayeke*   [˙ . .]   let him come
    ayeke   [˙ ˙ .]   do not let him come

(4) *lisaka*   [. . .]   a puddle, a marsh
    lisaka   [. . ˙]   a promise
    lisaka   [. ˙ ˙]   a poison

(5) *bosongo*   [. . .]   copper, brass
    bosongo   [. . ˙]   the river current
    bosongo   [. ˙ ˙]   a pestle for pounding food

In spite of constant attempts to speak Kele with a correct accent, I must have been guilty many a time of asking a boy to 'paddle for a book' or to 'fish that his friend is coming'! At Yakusu I heard the native head master reprimand a group of small children recently arrived in the school because they had been praying:

may Thy Kingdom not come, may Thy will not be done on earth as it is in heaven.

They were using a wrong tonal pattern for the verb forms as is seen in example (3) above. They had probably been taught this wrong pattern by non-Lokele teachers who were not familiar with the correct tonal structure of the Kele language. The words for fiancée and rubbish-pit are written the same (*liala*), but the tonal pattern of the former is [. ˙ .] while of the latter [. . .]. It is not difficult to imagine the consequences of using these words with wrong intonation![1]

Not all African languages have this essential tonal structure. In Ngwana, for instance, while there is a marked tonal pattern to the language, yet it is comparatively simple and is not of the same complicated nature as that which we have noted for Kele. The majority of words are like *amekuya* (p. 17) in that the last syllable but one has a high tone while all the others are low. This tonal structure gives Ngwana a peculiar lilting sound so that it is very easy to distinguish this language when it is being spoken in the babel of tongues on a Congo market-place. In some West African languages such as Mandinka, it is reported that tone patterns which were originally of importance in the language are now being dropped, possibly owing to the spreading of the language as a trade language used by other tribes. That the usage of an African language by members of other tribes does lead to changes in tonal patterns is certainly possible. I have myself noted wrong tonal patterns being used by men of the Mbae tribe when speaking in Kele. But it is far less common to hear wrong tonal patterns from the lips of Africans than from European learners of African tongues because the African will recognize the importance of getting correct tone in his speech whereas the European often does not realize the necessity for this.

---

[1] Note also the following sentences:
  alambaka boili [˙ . ˙ ˙ . . .] he watched the river-bank
  alambaka boili [˙ ˙ ˙ ˙ . ˙ .] he boiled his mother-in-law!

CHAPTER III

THE DRUMS

A SURPRISINGLY large variety of drums can be used to beat out the drum languages. Only one form is usually employed in any one region of Africa but these forms vary considerably in different parts of the continent. In later chapters we shall see that instruments other than drums can also serve to send out messages in the drum language. It is convenient to divide the drum types into two main groups:

A. all-wooden drums, hollowed out through a longitudinal slit so as to give two lips which are beaten to obtain two distinct notes; and

B. drums with skin tops which are used in pairs, one drum giving a high note and the other a lower note.[1]

A. *All-wooden drums.* The simplest kind of talking drum is the type used by the Lokele and surrounding tribes in the Stanleyville area of Belgian Congo. It is made from a solid log of reddish wood, hollowed out through a long narrow slit cut in the length of the log so that it looks like a gigantic cylindrical money-box (Fig. 2). Wherever this type of drum occurs in Central Africa it is nearly always the same species of wood which is used to make it; namely *Pterocarpus Soyauxii,* the tree from which many Central African tribes obtain a reddish powder by scraping the wood with oil (they then use this powder to adorn their bodies at dances and other social functions). The following account of the making of a Lokele talking drum may be of interest (25):

There are no special rites connected with present-day drum making. A log is ready for use when it has lain on the forest

---

[1] In ethnological nomenclature it is more accurate to restrict the name *drum* to type B and to call instruments of type A *gongs* or *slit-gongs.* In this book (which is a popular account of the drum languages rather than a strictly scientific study), however, the word *drum* is retained for all instruments because of its common usage in this way by writers from whom quotations are made. It is also inconvenient for our present purpose to have to distinguish as *gong* languages and *drum* languages what are essentially the same linguistic phenomenon. For the sake of clarity we shall refer to the *gongs* as *slit-drums* or *wooden drums* and to the *drums* as *skin-topped drums.* Words such as *drummer, drumsticks, drumming, drum language,* etc. can thus refer to either type of transmitting instrument.

floor for a sufficiently long time to allow the rotten, yellowish sap-wood to be removed from the hard, red heart-wood. The drum maker first chisels out a narrow, longitudinal slit in the length of the cylindrical log. This slit is deepened until it

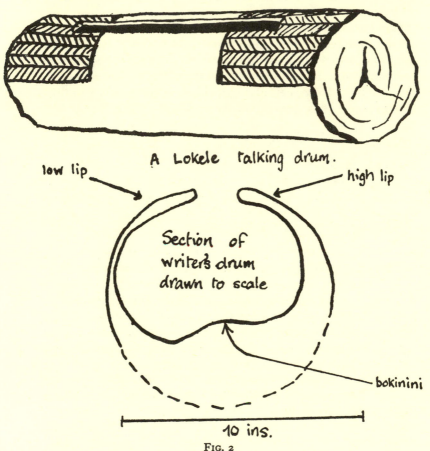

A Lokele talking drum.

low lip

high lip

Section of
writer's drum
drawn to scale

bokinini

10 ins.

FIG. 2

penetrates about half-way into the log. The interior of the drum is then hollowed out on both sides of the primary slit. The work is done by an adze, *fali*, sometimes assisted by a curved axe blade, *fondo*. The wooden chips produced are removed via the primary slit unless an accident to the end-wall of the drum leads to this becoming perforated and thus allowing of the removal of the chips through the hole so formed. In cases such as this the hole at the end is closed later by a circular bung. The hollowing on the two sides of the primary slit is differential, one side becoming thinner-walled and hollower than the other. The hollower side when struck near the slit gives a lower note than the other side. These two notes are distinguished as *limiki lya otolome* (voice of the male) and *limiki lya otomali* (voice of the female) for the high and low notes respectively. Many drums have a ridge of wood immediately below the slit separating the two hollowed sides of the drum. This ridge is called the back-bone (*bokinini*) of the drum. Figures 2 and 3 show a drum of this

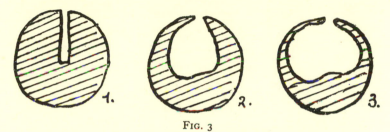

FIG. 3

Diagram showing stages in the hollowing of a Lokele slit-drum

kind and also a cross-section which demonstrates the difference in the hollowing beneath the two lips of the talking drum. This type of drum is called *boungu* or *bongungu* by the Lokele people, *bongongo* in Nkundo, *akungu* in Mbane, *ngonga* in Ngala.

The use of the words male and female to designate the two lips of the drum deserves some comment, for a perusal of the writings of different students on drum languages would seem to show a contradiction here, some stating that the low-toned note is female (as above) while others give the low-toned note a male designation. Actually such a difference is observed in one tribe; the account given above is based on the manufacture of a small drum with highly pitched notes; whereas if names are asked for the lips of the huge talking drums to be found in many Lokele villages, the low note will be given as male and the high note as female. The explanation seems to be that Africans (at any rate those living in the Stanleyville area) do not distinguish between two musical notes as 'high' and 'low', as do Europeans. Rather do they differentiate forcefulness and gentleness of musical timbre, or 'bigness' and 'littleness'.

I have often used the European conception of 'high' and 'low' when making inquiries into drum timbre or into other musical questions with Africans and my queries have met with a lack of comprehension. The mistake, of course, has been my own, because I have equated highness and lowness, which have an essen-

FIG. 4

A South Congo slit-drum with sections to show internal hollowing

tially spacial significance for African people with the pitch of a note produced at the same point in the human body whether it is high or low in tone, or produced at the same level on the talking drum. Maleness on the drum is the equivalent of 'bigness' or forcefulness, while femaleness represents 'littleness' or gentleness of timbre. In the small drum referred to above it is the high note which is more powerful and penetrates more easily, while with the big village drums the low note is usually more penetrating and audible at greater distances than the high note. The apparent discrepancy or inaccuracy in the accounts of the African names for the lips of the drum thus resolves itself into a lack of appreciation by the critic of African metaphor, or rather the carrying over of European metaphor into African modes of thought where it does not exist.

Slightly different forms of this same drum are seen in neighbouring areas of Congo. Thus in the Mayombe area to the west, the cylindrical form is replaced by a shape more like that of a Gladstone bag, with the slit along the top of the bag. Drums of the Mbae tribe may be of the type described for the Lokele or else have holes in each side and no backbone. Farther to the north the rounded base of the drum may be carved away to form a single or multiple stand, so that the drum rests on legs.

A rather different type of talking drum is that found in the south-east of Congo where it is called *mondo, kyondo, tfiondo.* Here the cylindrical log of wood, often of a whitish wood inferior for drum making to the red wood of the central area, bears two circular or rectangular holes joined by a very narrow slit. The hollowing-out practised beneath the lips of the drum and between the two openings is quite different from that in the Lokele drum type. Figure 4 shows how this hollowing is done. But, as in the first type described, the two lips when beaten give out two distinct notes, one high and the other low in pitch.

Another all-wooden talking drum, which shows a much more restricted area of distribution than the other types described, is the wedge-shaped slit-drum. Hollowing of this drum again leads to the production of differently pitched notes according to the place at which the drum is beaten. The total number of different notes produced on this drum may be as many as six (three for each side of the drum) but for talking purposes only two notes are used, often on one side only of the drum.

B. *Skin-topped drums.* Drums of this kind are common throughout Africa and are found in many areas where the all-wooden type is used exclusively for signalling purposes. In Central Africa for instance, where the types of wooden drums described above are used to transmit messages, the skin drum, *ngɔma,* is used for accompanying dancing. In east and south Central Africa the skin-topped drums are used also for signalling, but they probably rely on codes which are essentially different from the drum languages that form the subject of this book. Such signals may be sent out by a single drum on one note alone (which immediately shows that we are dealing with a mode of communication different from that used by the Lokele people) or in whole orchestras.

But skin-topped drums are used for transmitting drum languages by the Ashanti and Ewe peoples of West Africa. Here two drums are used together, one giving a high and the other a low note.

Customs associated with the drums. In our account of Lokele drum manufacture we were careful to point out that no rites seemed to be a necessary part of the carving of the drum. Women as a rule do not use the drum although they understand its messages, but,

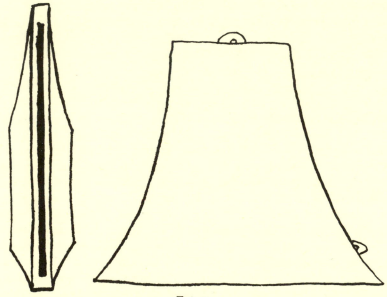

FIG. 5
Wedge-shaped slit-drum.   Kasai area

so far as can be discovered, there is no taboo against a woman beating the talking drum. In some parts of Africa, however, the drums seem to have a magical significance and are the objects of definite taboos and ceremonies. The Ashanti skin-topped drums, for instance, must not be 'harmed' by the proximity of blood in any form or skulls and jaw-bones. In the case of the huge slit-drums used by the Jibaro Indians of South America (although here we have what is really signalling with a code rather than by means of a drum language)

the drum maker in his tedious task must abstain from food for several days so as to have a stomach like an empty barrel (KARSTEN, 20. p. 109).

26

The story is told of one talking drum of the slit-drum type in Nigeria where the townspeople were so pleased at having a drum larger than any other in the surrounding villages that the maker was sacrificed and his blood sprinkled on the drum so that he should never be able to make, for a rival community, a drum of more imposing dimensions (BASDEN, 13. p. 360).

In some cases there is a special drummer for sending out messages and he alone is allowed to beat the talking drum. This must have been the case in Lokele country before the interest in talking on the drum began to decline. Writing in 1910 about Yakusu Sutton Smith said:

> the chief and his near relatives hold this privilege almost exclusively (referring to the operating of the drum).

But to-day, anyone in Yakusu could beat the drum without censure from the village elders. In the neighbouring Mbɔlɛ tribe there is sometimes found, however, a kind of hierarchy in drum beating. In each large village or group of villages one man has the priority of drum beating. He may or may not be the 'chief' as recognized by Government but he most probably represents the hereditary chief of the group of people concerned.[1] He usually has a stereotyped 'call-signal', each man in the neighbourhood with this priority on the drum having a different number of beats in his call-signal and so being recognized by his hearers whenever he beats out messages. When such a man wishes to send an important message he first of all beats out his call-signal on the village drum, or gets someone else to do this for him. Thereafter, until the end of the message no other drummer must beat a drum under pain of being heavily fined. Should another message be in process of being sent out, it must stop until the 'priority message' has gone through. This system is not found in other groups of the Stanleyville area, but as one listens to a drum message from one part of a village while other sections of the same village

---

[1] In this connection it is interesting to recall that the late M. FELIX EBOUÉ, the Governor-General of French Equatorial Africa, insisted in his book, *La nouvelle politique indigène* (Brazzaville 1941), that Government should seek out the real chief of a community and use him for the official 'chief'. He says: '... le chef préexiste. Cette préexistence reste souvent inconnue de nous, et le plus difficile nous est parfois de découvrir le vrai chef ... Qu'on le découvre, qu'on le place au grand jour, qu'on l'honore et qu'on en fasse son éducation'.

The presence of customs such as those described for the ba Mbɔlɛ people would assist in this task of 'finding the chief'.

and other villages up- and down-river are also sending messages, the wisdom of the Mbɔlε procedure is evident.

A word is necessary about the sticks used for beating the talking drum. These are usually constructed from the wood of a tree known for its resilience (Lokele men carve their canoe paddles from the wood of the same tree) and are tipped with a ball of rubber obtained from a forest creeper. The rubber strands are often held in place by a covering of cane-work. Sometimes a piece of palm-frond is used or even an ordinary stick; but these latter are detrimental to the talking drum and liable to crack the lips with much usage. A Lokele drummer would be most annoyed if anything other than the proper rubber-covered sticks were used on his drum.

For beating the huge signalling gongs of the South Sea Islands wooden clubs are used or sometimes bundles of rattan cane. Sounds may even be produced in some areas by kicking the drum lips. But it should be noted again that signalling on these gongs seems to be different in kind from the talking drum messages of Africa; only one lip of the South Sea Island gongs is used for message transmission whereas African talking drums have two lips each of which has a different sound.

In some descriptions of drum talking writers have been at pains to indicate which hand was employed for beating out a given syllable. But this is not usually a significant point. The two lips of the drum give out the same notes wherever they are struck, whether by the right or by the left hand. Interchanging of hands during the beating-out of a message is only effected in order to help the drummer to send his message smoothly and without halting. Different drummers beat the same message in different ways so far as the use of left and right hands is concerned. Sometimes two consecutive notes on the same lip are beaten with the same hand (but this is not necessarily the case). A one-handed man would not be obliged to give up drum signalling! We have been told that if a woman were to beat a message on a Lokele drum she would only be allowed one drumstick with which to do so. The message so beaten out would be intelligible, but it would have an 'accent' characteristic of an incompetent operator. Usually a drummer stands behind the high-toned lip of the drum and beats out his message with the low-toned lip away from him. But Lokele drummers who attain real proficiency at the art often drum with the low-toned lip near to them and the high-toned lip away. To do so means, of course, a reversal of the gestures made by the drummer and success in beating in this way is regarded as a criterion of excellence in drum beating.

Times of beating; distance of travel. The best conditions for drum beating usually obtain in the early morning or late evening. There are two main reasons for this. During the day the many noises of the village and occupations of the people prevent messages from being audible except for short distances. And secondly, the heating effect of the sun's rays striking the ground causes air movements in an upward direction (the air over the village square often shimmers in the noon heat) and these currents tend to carry the sound away from the ground. Sound seems to carry better over water and it is noticeable how each Lokele village invariably arranges its largest drums on the top of the river bank perpendicular with the beach and with the low-toned lip facing up-river. For communication with inland forest villages however, smaller drums are often used of a shriller timbre; these have no definite orientation.

In reports of the distances over which drums can be heard, it is probable that writers have confused messages drummed out by a single drum and those in which messages have been relayed from one village to another. Hence we read statements of this kind

> . . . when a sudden hush falls over the great forest they (the drums) can be heard, so it is asserted, for sixty miles . . . (POWELL, E. A., *The Map that is half unrolled*. London 1926, p. 128).

This assertion surely refers to a series of five or six drums and not to a single instrument. The following quotations give a much sounder picture of the actual facts and agree with conditions found in the Yakusu district:

(*a*) for the pigmy tribes of French Equatorial Africa:
in the morning and in the evening during calm weather without wind, the war tom-tom is heard for a distance of eleven kilometres.[1]

(*b*) for Nigeria:
the beating of an ikolo can be heard up to a distance of five miles.[2]

[1] TRILLES, R. P., *Les Pygmées de la forêt équatoriale*, Paris 1931.
[2] BASDEN, 13. p. 359.

(c) for the South Sea Islands:
   people can recognize the gong of a particular individual at a
   distance of six miles.[1]

One of the largest of the baEna drums, situated in the village of
Lesali at the foot of Stanley Falls can be heard at the village of
Yatuka which is more than twenty miles downstream. But messages are rarely sent as far as this; the working distance of a Lokele
drum is usually about six or seven miles at night-time and four or
five miles during the day.

Much greater distances than those attained by a single drum
can be covered by relaying the messages from one village to
another. This does not occur unless the message is of very great
importance. It would be quite feasible to institute a system
of drum telephony in a Central African country like the Belgian
Congo, but the organism arranging such a system would have to
secure special operators who would remain by the drums to
receive and send on messages. The ordinary African village
drummer could not be relied upon to do this. For the apathy of
the African village drummer towards anything which does not
directly concern him would militate against the message getting
through. The passage of H. M. Stanley down the river through
Lokele country in 1877 was certainly heralded by relayed drum
messages from Lokele drummers; but in this case there was something of great moment to all the community: strange black men
and stranger white-skinned men in canoes quite different from
those used by Lokele fishermen and paddled by men who turned
their backs to the direction the canoe was taking. And, above all,
the possibility of meat to those who could capture one or more of
the intruders! But it would be difficult to get a response from dis-
tant villages if, for example, we wished to call a certain man living
sixty miles away, to come up to the Station.

Another great obstacle to the relaying of drum messages over
great distances is the fact of the tribal nature of most drum
languages. Since the drum language is based on the tribal tongue
it is usually understood only by members of the tribe. There is
no 'international' drum language in Africa any more than there
is a common spoken language.[2] At Yakusu it is possible to hear
drums beating in four quite different drum languages any day.

[1] RUTTER, O., *The Pagans of North Borneo*, London 1929.
[2] The widely-used 'trade languages' have no counterpart on the drum.

So that at the boundary of the tribal group sending out a message there would be a check in transmission. This check could only be overcome if a drummer were available who understood the drum language of his own and of the neighbouring tribe. Such men do occur in boundary villages. Children of parents who come from two different tribes often learn both languages and become bilingual on the drum. But they are not numerous and this fact makes it difficult to relay a drum message across the boundary of the tribe. Thus, many of the stories of news travelling across vast areas of Africa in a very short time must be accepted with great reserve even although the drum language may seem to provide an explanation.

CHAPTER IV

HOW MESSAGES ARE SENT ON THE TALKING DRUM

Europeans have often been amazed at the speed of messages . . . and no amount of questioning has elicited the 'secret' of the means of communication. It is only secret because it is so simple and so patent. (GOODWIN, I. p. 232.)

WE have seen how many Central African languages are tonal, that is to say, each syllable of the words spoken has one of two fundamental tones, either high or low, and must be given this tone wherever it occurs in a word or sentence. Moreover, the African slit-drums used to transmit messages have two notes, high and low, when struck at different points; the skin-topped drums which are also used to transmit the drum language are used in pairs so that one drum is high in tone and the other low. Comparing these facts about the drum language and the instruments of transmission it is not difficult to 'jump to the conclusion' that the basis of the drum languages of Africa is the tonal pattern of the words which make up the languages. This is the case. What is drummed out is the tonal pattern of the words which make up the drum language. This so-called drum language is essentially the same as the spoken language of the tribe.

Let us illustrate this principle with some examples from the Lokele drum. The Kele word for father is *sango* (· ·) for mother is *nyango* (. ·) and for child is *wana* (· .). These words are all found in the drum language. Whenever they occur, *sango* is represented by two beats on the high-toned lip, H H, *nyango* is given a beat on the low lip followed by a beat on the high lip, L H, while *wana* has a beat on the high lip followed by a beat on the low lip, H L. All three words occur in the drum name for an orphan; you can pick them out and see how the drum beats correspond with the tonal patterns of the words.

drummed:	H	L	LH	L	H H	L	L H
tones:	[·	.	. ·	.	· ·	.	. ·]
spoken:	*wana*	*ati*	*la*	*sango*		*la*	*nyango*
meaning:	child	has	no	father		nor	mother

Notice, too, that the tones and the method of beating the word *la* are the same in the two places where this occurs in the message-sentence.

In the first example of spoken Kele which we gave (on p. 17) the word *asooya* (he has come) occurred. This word is also an element of the Kele drum language and on the drum it is represented by a succession of beats L H L H. Comparing these with the tones given on p. 17, it is clear that the drum beating is simply following the tonal pattern of the word.[1]

The story of drum signalling, however, is not quite so simple as that already given. The reader will probably have formed one objection to the account so far rendered; namely, that there must be a large number of Kele words with the same tonal pattern as that of *sango* and others like *nyango* or *wana*. If only the tonal patterns are drummed out, how can such words be distinguished on the drum? Working through the Kele dictionary used by the missionaries of the B.M.S. at Yakusu we find that there are some one hundred and thirty words which have the same tonal form as *sango*, while more than two hundred are tonally like *nyango*.[2] These words, if they occur in the drum language, must have exactly the same beats on the drum. But they are distinguished in another way.

Let us take a series of words with the same tone pattern as *sango*, namely, words which occur in the drum language. Such are: *songe* (··) the moon; *kɔkɔ* (··) the fowl; and *fele* (··) a kind of fish.

Whenever one of these three words is used on the drum it is always accompanied by a number of other words which, together with it, make a little phrase. Thus:

[· · · · · ·]
the moon: *songe li tange la manga*; drummed: H H L H L L L L
            the moon looks down at the earth

[·· · · · · ··]
the fowl: *kɔkɔ olongo la bokiokio*; drummed: H H L H H L L H L H L
            the fowl, the little one which says '*kiokio*'

[1] Stress is also important in the drumming out of the message, as mentioned on p. 16, But tone is more important than stress and is the real basis of the drum language broadcast.
[2] The words referred to here are mainly noun forms. If verbal forms were included the numbers of words tonally like *sango* and *nyango* would be very much increased.

[. ·· . . ·· .]

the fish *fele*: *yafele la yamboku*; drummed: L H H L L H L
    all the *fele*-fish and all the *mboku*-fish

Clearly, although the words we have chosen have the same tonal patterns, yet when they are accompanied by the other words which explain them the total tonal patterns are characteristic and quite different from others.

Here is another series of words which, although similar in tonal pattern, yet because they are never drummed singly but always included in short sentences or phrases, are not confused by the Lokele drummer or listener.

manioc;   spoken: *lomata* (...); drummed: *lomata otikala la kondo*
                                    L LLLHLL L HL
    manioc remains in deserted garden

plantain;   spoken: *likɔndɔ* (...); drummed: *likɔndɔ libotumbela*
                                      LL LHLH LL
    plantain which is propped up (when ripe)

the forest; spoken: *lokonda* (...); drummed: *lokonda teketeke*
                                    L L LLLLL
    forest ? (this word is of doubtful significance)

up above; spoken: *likolo* (...);[1] drummed: *likolo ko nda use*
                                    L L L L HHH
    above in the sky.

Again, a comparison of the complete tonal patterns of the small phrases in which the similarly toned words occur shows that there is complete differentiation on the drum.

We have a parallel in some of our European hymn tunes which begin with the same few notes but later are quite distinguishable because of the varied melody of the notes of succeeding bars. (Fig. 6)

Note that this parallel with European hymn tunes only holds for the musical part of the hymn. Whereas in the drum language the drummed melody follows exactly the tonal pattern of the words, in the hymn tune there is no attempt to follow any tonal pattern inherent in the words of the hymn. As we have seen earlier, European languages do not have the same kind of tonal structure as African tongues. But in the case of a few melodies

[1] Note: *lokonda* and *likolo* do occur without these words accompanying them in certain other characteristic phrases.

this sort of correspondence is seen. Compare, for instance, the normal way of saying: *I'm coming*, with the tonal pattern given to those words in the plantation song: 'Poor Old Joe'. They show a marked resemblance. This may be a coincidence, of course, but it is of interest that it occurs in a song associated with men of African descent.

FIG. 6

N.B. All tunes are transposed to key F to facilitate comparison.

The drum phrases. The few examples of drum phrases already given (manioc, plantain, forest, up above, orphan) may have served to show that there is a good deal of interesting material in these proverb-like words. They can give a foreigner, and especially the European, a real insight into native modes and expressions. Agricultural operations with manioc and plantain can be deduced from the drum names for these commodities. Manioc is a crop which takes about a year to grow and so, in the fertile forest region, the garden is covered with a rank growth of weeds before the roots of the manioc are ready to be harvested. The heavy fruit bunches of the plantain, which with manioc form the staple diet of Central African communities, will overturn the plant in a tropical storm unless they are propped up by a stout forked stick.

More Kele drum phrases are now given, together with comments on their meaning and value for help in understanding native thought and customs.

wife: *bokali la balanga*

    L H H L L L   L

> The word *bokali* in spoken Kele means *a tail*; but we are doubtful whether this indicates that the wife is considered to be a mere appendage of the male in Lokele-land! Rather is it probable that *bokali* is an older form of the present-day word for *wife*, namely *wali*.
> *balanga* means yams, so that the drum name emphasizes a woman's culinary duties . . . '*the woman with yams*'.

girl: *boseka botilakɛndɛ linginda*

    L L L H H L L H L L L

i.e. '*the girl will never go to the linginda (fishing net)*'

> As in many other African communities, there is a strict division of labour in Lokele country. Fishing with certain types of nets is only done by the men.

witch-doctor: *kanga simba elɔkitɔ ya olongo lolikalika*

    L L H H L L H L L L H H H L L L L

i.e. '*the witch-doctor, lion, of the dance*'

> The meaning of *elɔkitɔ* I have not been able to discover, many users of the words being unable to translate it. The remainder of the phrase shows the power of the witch-doctor (the 'lion') and the close connection between his profession and dancing.

money: *bilanga tuka bolonja mbeko*

    L H H H H L L L H L

the pieces of metal which arrange palavers

> In some Lokele villages there are blacksmiths who make hoes, knives and spears. Scraps of metal were left beneath the forges and these fused with the heat to form pieces used as money or ornaments. Fines involving these tokens were a common sanction of Central African courts before the white man came.

war: *bitei bilamba fuko*

    H L H H L   L L L

war watches for opportunities

As explained later in connection with another drum phrase, surprise is one of the most important elements of Central African military strategy.

corpse: *bolio wa bakalekale ko nda bauki ko nda nyɛlɛ*
LHL H L LH LH L H LH L L H LL
the corpse lying on its back on the clods of earth

This needs little comment, but it shows the rather poetical nature of the drum phrases. It is not enough to say that the corpse is 'on the ground' (*ko nda nyɛlɛ*) but we must say 'on the clods on the ground'. Such a duplication of information is to be found in a number of other phrases.

small fish: *yafele la yamboku ya otomali wa lio*
LHH L L H L H LL HH L HL
the fish of the women-folk

Again is seen the duplication of the names of the two kinds of fish. The addition of the name for a woman shows that the fish is small and beneath the attention of the menfolk.

goat: *imbumbuli fa okenge*
L H LL H L H H
the little goat of the village

This derogatory note is also observable in the drum language name for a goat in other regions. The Foma people call it:

mbuli olongo la fefe — the goat the son of the fool.

Because of its lack of strength and incapability of self-defence.

the drum itself: *bɔkɔkɔ wa olondo*
L L L H L L H
the log of the bolondo tree

Actually the red wood from which the Lokele drum is made is not the *bolondo* tree, which has a brown heartwood. Mbae tribesmen use *bolondo* for their drums, so that it is possible that Lokele drums were originally made of this wood, the discovery of the superior *wele* tree being made after the drum-name had become stereotyped.

More examples of these short, proverb-like phrases will be found in later chapters on the drum messages of various kinds. Enough examples have been given to show the way in which the sentences reflect the life of a Central African community and we can heartily endorse the words of a Belgian Government officer describing the drum language of the Luba tribe of South Congo:

> In my opinion these phrases are full of interest for anyone who wishes to become properly acquainted with the mentality of the native peoples. They (the phrases) can help in understanding ideas and customs which to us appear inexplicable and can provide us with unexpected and hitherto unknown points of view (VERBEKEN, 32. p. 721).

We have already come across a number of words in the drum phrases quoted which have a doubtful or definitely unknown significance, or which show a form that differs from the present-day spoken form of the word. This has also been observed in other African drum languages. It seems that the drum language, consisting as it does of stereotyped phrases, has perpetuated words which have been forgotten or fallen into disuse in the more flexible spoken language, just as some old English writings, e.g. Chaucer's works and even our English Bible, preserve words which are not heard in twentieth-century conversation. When I have been anxious to get to know the meaning of certain words in the drum language and have questioned Lokele drummers, I have often met with the reply: 'These words were given to us by our fathers and we do not understand what they mean.' Obviously, for the student of African linguistics, these archaic words of the drum language have the same kind of interest as the words of an ancient document for students of the origins of English.

The examples quoted of the drum phrases have been mainly concerned with the names of things. But verbal forms must also have a stereotyped pattern as a rule. Thus, instead of saying: 'he has returned', the poetic drum speech says: 'he has brought back his legs, he has brought back his feet'. Duplication is again noticeable here. Similarly for: 'he has arrived', the drum says: 'he has put his feet down, he has put his legs down'. Here are the words used:

he has returned: *asooinola batindi mbisa, asooinola bakolo mbisa*
          L HLLHH L H H   H L LHLLHH L L L   H L

he has arrived: *aseli batindi bakolo se*

LLH LHH L L L H

'Don't worry', which in spoken Kele would be translated by some verbal form as *owangeke* (don't be afraid) must on the drum be given quite a long sentence as:

seleke likɔkɔ lya botema se   put the knot of the heart down

LHH L L H H L H L H

or:

sokolaka likɔkɔ lya botema   take away the knot of the heart,

L H H H L L H H L H L

likolo ko nda use   up into the air

L LL L   H HH

These examples should suffice to explain the principle enunciated at the beginning of the chapter, namely, that the drum language is essentially not different from the spoken language and that it is the tonal patterns of characteristic short phrases which are actually drummed out on the two lips of the two-toned talking drum or on the two skin-topped drums of West Africa.

CHAPTER V

WHAT'S IN A NAME?

La voix du 'tshiondo' est vraiment impressionante. Elle semble être la voix de la nature même, de la nature primitive et sauvage. Et parfois elle se confond avec le souffle de la nuit mystérieuse et devient comme l'écho des siècles passées. (VERBEKEN, 32. p. 258.)

IN all drum-signalling communities every male member of the tribe has a drum name. This is given to him by his father, sometimes after a special ceremony such as the initiation ceremony, or sometimes, as with Lokele boys, as soon as the lad is old enough to understand the drum (that is, when he is five or six years old). In the Mbole forest the drum name given to a young boy is changed at the initiation ceremony when he becomes a 'man'.

A full drum name in the Stanleyville district of Congo is a lengthy affair and consists of three parts:

(a)   a name characteristic of the boy himself, this corresponding perhaps with our Christian name;

(b)   a portion which is really the characteristic part (a) of the boy's father's drum name;

(c)   a final phrase representing the name of the village from which the boy's mother came.

Hence two boys with the same mother and father will have parts (b) and (c) identical. But in the polygamous communities of Central Africa it frequently happens that two 'brothers' have names which differ in part (c). Parts (a) and (b) are joined by some word meaning son of: *litianga lieko lya*, or, *bolongo la*, while parts (b) and (c) have a joining word *bokana la*, or simply *wa* or *ya*. Parts (b) and (c) sometimes reverse their order.

Among tribes where the drum language is a deeply-rooted institution and not recently borrowed from drumming neighbours, the drum names are very rarely or never made up by a boy's father but are names inherited from ancestors of the boy's family; just as in many European families, Christian names are often passed down from generation to generation. But in the case of tribes such as the Mbae people where the drum is obviously not a tribal institution, but has been taken over from drumming Lokele and bAngwa neighbours, these drum names may be new ones made up for the newcomer. There is no doubt, for instance, of the recentness (post-European colonization period) of the drum name of Ekbulu, one of the Mission overseers in the Mbae area:

> *kulɔgɛ e' dwa' be osongo tene*   *might comes to nought in the white man's*
> HHHH L H L L H HH   *town*
>> which, being interpreted, means that no matter how strong you may be in the eyes of fellow-Africans your power counts for little when confronted with the white man.

Often enough, however, the full drum name with its three component parts is not drummed out. (We Europeans, too, reserve our full names for filling in passport forms and identity cards!) The first or 'Christian' name is usually considered sufficient to characterize a man. For the sake of interest, however, we give the full name of Boyele, a drum maker from the Lokele village of Yafɔlɔ.

(a) *loola lokoki bolongo la*   the spitting cobra whose virulence never abates, son of

(b) *bolemba ko la yeto ya*   the bad spirit with the spear; *likonga bokana wa*   mother's town

(c) *batɔ baaka la loola*   Yangɔndɛ, i.e. the men who *lokoki lwa bainatende*   were as the spitting cobra whose poison never abates, related to the baEna people

To show how these drum names are handed down we have added the names on the drum of Baofa, Boyele's grandfather, Litumanya, Boyele's father and Litumanya II, Boyele's son, now a schoolboy in the author's school at Yakusu. The three former were all professional drum makers (*see* Fig. 7).

It will be seen that the present-day schoolboy has inherited both the spoken and the drum name of his grandfather. His grandfather's mother and his own mother, however, were not from the same village and so the latter part of the drum names are not identical. Similarly, Boyele and his grandfather had identical 'Christian names' on the drum.

Just as the small stereotyped phrases for the names of objects

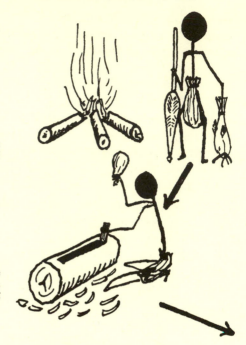

ḄAOFA:
 Spitting cobra whose virulence never abates

LITUMANYA I:
 The bad spirit with the spear; mother's village, Ifiti; son of spitting cobra

on the drum are of interest in throwing light on African customs, so too these personal drum names and the similar village drum names are able to give the student an insight into the 'Weltanschauung' of the Central African native. Here are some picturesque names of men or boys who have been connected with the Yakusu Boys' School:

Botikotiko, a teacher at a Mission Rural School:

bowango bokatomeli ita   *the strong man has not yet been sent to fight*

(but when he does go . . . he will be ready!)

Wawina, a medical assistant in Stanleyville:

efefe etilaoke njasɔ   *the proud man will never listen to advice*

This name, by the way, would not be resented by any of our African boys by whom independence of action and even insolence to superiors are regarded as expressions of power.

42

Lotika, also a medical assistant:

wana ati la sango la nyango *the child has no father or mother, he*
a lombakeli yeka ya bituka   *awaits food in the communal talking-*
             house

That is, he gets food when and where he can.

Bofomo, a house-boy of the author.

osɛkɛlɛkɛ lokomba lwindo *don't laugh at the black skin for a*
twɛlɔ twa akɛnɛnɛ nyongo *black skin belongs to everyone*
lokomba lwindo lotisandelo
boto se

This name is obviously pre-European civilization!

It will be noticed that in the above examples the spoken name

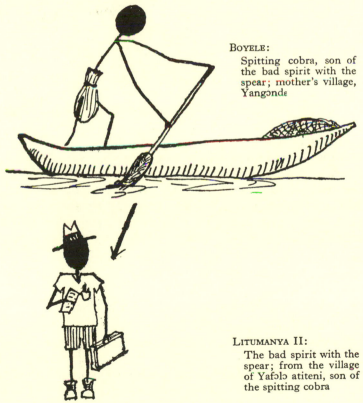

BOYELE:
 Spitting cobra, son of the bad spirit with the spear; mother's village, Yangɔndɛ

LITUMANYA II:
 The bad spirit with the spear; from the village of Yafɔlɔ atiteni, son of the spitting cobra

FIG. 7
Drum names of Boyele's family

43

and the drummed name have nothing in common, except in the case of Lotika, which means in spoken Kele, an orphan. But in other tribes the spoken name is often the first word of the drum name. Thus for another teacher in the service of the Mission, this time a man from the nearer baMbɔle tribe:

(a)	*mɛnɛokenge la yeto ya ilondo*	owner of the town with the sheathed knife
(b)	*kumi la likanda lya yaatelia*	elder of the country called yaatelia
(c)	*bokana wa yaolonga liɔnga*	mother's town, Yaolonga

We inscribe this teacher's name on our registers as Meneokenge.

Because drum names are inherited from ancestors of the clan it is impossible for a stranger to obtain a real drum name in Lokele country. I myself sought for a name by means of which to be distinguished on the drum from the many other white people in Lokele-land. But I was asked for my father's name on the drum, a request which it was impossible to meet. Some tribesmen refused to believe that I had no drum name in Europe or that my father had not been given such a name. Being unfamiliar with any language other than a tonally constructed one, they cannot understand why Europeans do not use a drum and have even interpreted my inability to give my drum name in French as a refusal on my part to tell them about the Belgian drum language! In early days, pioneer missionaries and other Europeans were given native names, often those of some tribal elder, recently dead. In such a case a drum name would be possible for the white man, because he could take the drum name of his native namesake. This practice, however, is obsolete at Yakusu although still extant at some other B.M.S. stations down the river. The problem of giving me a drum name was not solved until I proffered the information that my father was a member of an English country-dance team. Then it was easy:

bosongo olimo ko nda lokonda	the white man (*see* p. 49)
ekɛsɛ olongo lolikalika	if he dances
likolo ko nda use	up into the sky (reference to arm and leg movements)
batɔ ba oki kosɛkɛ twɛlɔ	men of the village will laugh
caa caa	ha! ha!

bakenene ko nda ɔnɔkɔ   pains in the mouth
wa olongo lolikalika   of the dancer

It is perhaps hardly complimentary to English country-dancing to have given rise to a name of this kind, in which the part of the choreographic expert consists in making people laugh until they ache! But such is the atmosphere of the African dance.

Girls and women do not have special drum names like men and boys. They are always referred to on the drum by the name of the man, father or husband, to whom they 'belong'. Thus a girl is:

boseka botilakɛndɛ linginda lya plus the drum name of her father
(*see* p. 36)

while a wife is:

bokali la alanga wa plus the drum name of the husband

Villages and sections of villages have drum names, as has already been mentioned in connection with part (*c*) of the drum name for a man or boy. Some boundary villages rejoice in two names, one on the drum of one tribe (often rather a derogatory name on the 'foreigner's' drum) and another on the drum of the other tribe. The study of these village drum names is fascinating because they often reveal some historical incident referring to the people of the village. For instance the following drum names are replete with historical significance:

Yakusu: *bafaka ko la alɛmbu·* (the older generation were) soft as fish floats in war

Yatumbo: *baaka la likundo* they were with revenge

Yatuka: *baaka bangɛnɛ liande* they were masters of the river

Yangambi: *bɔkɔlika ko nda olombo* the chimpanzee of the bOlombo folk

    This village had a feud with neighbouring Lokele villages on the south bank of the river and as a result moved over to the north bank into territory occupied by the forest Olombo tribe. Lokele people refer to these forest people as monkeys and hence the derogatory name for Yangambi.

A schoolmaster in Africa soon learns to distinguish among members of different tribes and even of different villages. The people of a village section are all descendants of a common ancestor and hence are likely to possess similar psychological traits. Soon after I had taken over the charge of the Yakusu Boys' School I recognized as rather proud and irritable natures the boys coming from the village of Yalɔkɔmbɛ. Other missionaries shared in this opinion of the Yalɔkɔmbɛ youngsters. It was not surprising therefore to learn the drum name of this town:

> bolemba boti la oto la oto   the bad spirit has no friend nor kinsman

This name was not chosen by Yalɔkɔmbɛ people but was given to them by other Lokele villages as the result of a fairly recent feud (probably about 1880). The villages of Yalɔkɔmbɛ, Yaloca, Yaowamya and Yaliele were all originally on the right bank of the river (the north bank). But after a fight in which Yalɔkɔmbɛ challenged the rest of the villages, these latter moved away from the aggressors and went over to the south bank where they are still to be found. Before the fight Yalɔkɔmbɛ had the drum name:

> baaka lilole fosinga yeo   they had medicines to defeat curses

but the less complimentary name given above was attached to them and still remains.

The name for the country down-river is also of interest:

> liande lya loleka lotilesaelo   the river of poison whose virulence had no end

In the days before white civilization came into contact with Central African peoples, a man would never leave the territory of his own tribe or the tribe to which his mother belonged. There was no desire to broaden geographical knowledge by 'travel in foreign parts' among tribes with decided cannibal tendencies. This drum name for the down-river tribes reflects the dread with which the Central African native regarded members of unknown peoples. It is perhaps a little surprising to find that the Lokele folk feared the down-river end of their territory rather than the up-river portion. This may be partly due to the fact that Lokele and baEna tribesmen at Stanley Falls seem to be related in many ways (*see* p. 41 for the name of Yangɔndɛ, a central Lokele village). Moreover, the baEna folk, while speaking a language different from spoken Kele, have a drum language which is obviously the same as the Kele drum language. But another reason for the title given to the down-river tribes may be connected with river war-strategy. The most favoured method of raiding a riverine village was to begin from a base down-river from the victims. A land force was sent behind the village under cover of darkness while canoes crept stealthily up-river, keeping well into the bank. Then at dawn combined operations from land and water were directed against the unsuspecting villagers, and a quick get-away was made with the river-current back to the home town. Villages raiding down-river would thus have to contend with the river current in making a get-away, and this would be a very difficult operation to bring to a successful conclusion. An interesting sidelight on this point is the fact that most Lokele expansion has seemed to be up-river rather than down-river, except for the Yawembɛ section at the west which appears to have had an origin different from that of the other sections of the tribe.

'What's in a name?' is the somewhat cynical query of the product of Western civilization. To the African, names, whether spoken or drummed, are full of significance.

CHAPTER VI

OURSELVES AS OTHERS SEE US

O wad some power the giftie gie us
To see oursels as others see us!

WHEN Robert Burns wrote his famous lines he did not think of one possibility of obtaining the desired 'giftie', namely, of going to Central Africa, living there for some time among the native peoples and then listening carefully for the nicknames he would surely receive from them. The African, for whom European qualifications and titles of respect mean nothing, is very quick to seize upon some salient point in a stranger's character and from that to evolve a characteristic nickname. Sometimes these names are uncomplimentary, although friends of the man concerned rarely fail to see the justification for the spontaneous appellation. Sometimes, on the other hand, the names are of a kind that any man would covet for himself. Although Lokele tribesmen were wont, in the past, to give to Europeans the names of tribal elders, yet occasionally they coined a new name for a man. Who would not be envious of the name given to Wherrett, one of the Yakusu pioneer missionaries who died 'in harness' after only a short stay on the field? *akelaolau* — he did good. *Viangavianga* was the title received from Lower Congo natives by Comber, one of the earliest Protestant missionaries in the Congo. It means: one who is always feverishly busy. In those days, as to-day, there is so much to occupy a missionary's time that being busy is certainly a notable feature in the lives of those called to this work. Stanley's famous name of: *Bula Matale* — breaker of stones — reflects the amazement of the Bas-Congo natives when they saw that this great man who became the leader of the young *État Indépendant du Congo* was able to blast away the side of a mountain so as to give passage to a road destined to carry goods from the mouth of the river, through the cataract region, to the Pool and so to the centre of Africa.

But a spoken name is preferably short in form; we shorten Robert to Bob and Valentine to Val; in Lokele-land *Baelongandi* becomes *Baelo* and *Setefano* becomes *Sete*. The drum name on the other hand is necessarily long, for reasons we have already discussed, and may consist of a number of words. It thus has more

Mbac drummer calling chief who is
in the forest

Drums in the Drum-house, *ngwaka*, at Yafunga, a
Lokele village

interesting data than the spoken form for those who would seek to understand the meanings behind names.

Unfortunately we do not find individual names for Europeans on the talking drum, they are rather generic names representing the reactions of the people to a whole group of strangers. Thus, in Lokele country the name for the white man is:

| *bosongo olimo ko nda lokonda* | red as copper, spirit from the |
| L L L L H H L   H L L   L | forest |

Possibly the word *bosongo* given here is not the same as the word for copper (*see* p. 19); it may be the Lokele way of saying Swahili *mzungu* — white man — although the tonal derivation would not be easy in this latter case. But Lokele drummers have told me that the allusion is to the colour of the skin of the first white man they met. That he was a 'spirit-from-the-forest' indicates the sense of fear which held the first tribesmen who saw the intruder, for there is a belief extant to-day that he who sees a spirit in the forest will die as a result of his vision. The name serves to suggest the thought that the appellation: 'white man' may be a figment of European speech so far as some parts of Africa are concerned. Lokele people really call us *red*-men; the analogy for them is with copper and not chalk! — and is, after all, a nearer approach than whiteness to the actual colour of the nordic skin. We may add that the term red-man[1] as applied to their own people is an insult of the gravest kind and has led to fights innumerable in the Yakusu Boys' School.

Another point of interest about this name is that the drum name for the white man begins with *bosongo* [. . .] whereas the spoken form of the word for white man is *bosongo* [. . ·]. Notice the difference in tonal pattern. This is the only word I have been able to find in Kele where the drummed and spoken tone patterns appear to be different. But Lokele drummers tell me that the words are not really identical. When the white man was first seen he was given the name we have described above because of the strange colour of his skin. Later, however, he was seen to be very powerful; as powerful indeed as the river-current *bosongo* [. . ·] (*see* p. 19). So he came to be called *bosongo* [. . ·] in the spoken language of the tribe. But the stereotyped drum language had already fixed its name for the intruder and so continues to beat

[1] In the spoken language: *boto botelu*.

49

out *bosongo* [. . .] even when the more flexible spoken language has changed the tones used. This story is probably a rationalization of the situation rather than a real explanation of what actually occurred, but it is of interest in showing that Lokele drummers believe an explanation is required when tonal values of spoken and drummed words differ. It also suggests that the drum language is more conservative than the spoken language of the tribe.

Other names are found in other drum languages to describe the white man. The baMbɔlɛ tribe has a name for the European which reminds us of the part played by Stanley in the early days of Congo government. So widespread was his fame that all government officers became known as 'of *Bula Matale*'. Thus the State man in the baMbɔlɛ area is:

> *bosongo okumaka atale*   the white man sent by *Bula Matale*

A missionary going into this area has a slightly different name for he is sent, not by the State, but by the director of the Mission. The Rev. W. Millman, one of the Yakusu pioneer missionaries and director of the Mission for over thirty years, was called *Mokili* by the native people. Hence any missionary entering a baMbɔlɛ village is heralded by the drum as:

> *bosongo okumaka Okili*   the white man sent by *Mokili*
> Notice that the baMbɔlɛ elide the *M* which is usually retained by the Lokele people.

Luba tribesmen of the South Congo area drum out the name of the white man as:

> *kabukebuke kabakatuka*   ghost, returning from the place of
> *kudi bamfumuetu*   our chiefs

The Government officer reporting this believes that the allusion to 'ghost' has to do with the colour of the skin of the European. Experiences of my own in Lokele-land may, however, throw another light on to this drum name. When I have been engaged in drumming on Lokele drums in front of older members of the tribe I have often been told that I am simply one of their fore-fathers returned to the land of his origin from the home of the spirits. The latter gave me a white skin before I left them. The power of any B.M.S. missionary to speak the Kele language is explained by the belief that he is speaking his real mother tongue, for he was, in a former generation, a member of the tribe. Indeed,

European skill and science in inventing and flying aeroplanes or building and travelling in river steamers is due to the good favour of the spirits who have endowed former Africans with knowledge and ability at the same time as the white skin. Why should they come back to Africa were it not for the fact that they were once members of African tribes? So the Luba name we have quoted may indicate this belief, namely, that the white man has actually resided in the land of spirits with the chiefs of the tribe and that he is simply one of them returned under a new guise to lead the tribe in new ways.

In the drum language of the bAngwa tribe to the north of Stanleyville we find allusion to the power of the European as a colonist:

mengɛki wa likula limete   he to whom the land belongs

This name is probably one that was coined some time after the organization of European Government in the area.

Not so complimentary is the name reported from the Cameroons:

awo bode ntuk, awo bode ntuk he enslaves the people, he en-
                                                          slaves the people
alanne nnama nnome   which remain in the land

Two names are reported for the European by a missionary working on the drum language of the Tumba people, the first being:

ejim'ondele bosoka jokalaka   venerable white man, companion
                                                    of chiefs

This makes one feel that colonization has been a happy affair in this region. But the other name which this tribe use for the white man suggests that we have not all been seen in such an honourable light:

ikongo ifonge kukola   a stinging caterpillar is best left alone

As mentioned in an earlier paragraph, these names are generic names and apply to all white men in a given area. They are not personal appellations. When it is necessary to distinguish between, say, a State officer and a missionary, this can be done on the drum in ways which vary with the tribe. We have already noted that the baMbɔlɛ drum refers to the directors of the two men. In Kele the name already given for white man, namely:

bosongo olimo ko nda lokonda

is reserved for the State official. For the missionary this name is first drummed and an addition made of:

wa lokasa loa lonjwa	of the leaf used for roofing

The reference is to a leaf of a species of the Marantaceae which, because of its huge size and glabrous surface, makes excellent tiles for building up roofs on mud and even brick houses. The leaf is here compared with the Book — the Bible — which is to the fore in all Protestant missionary work. The aim of the missionary so to educate his church members that they may be able to read the Bible for themselves and have immediate access to its treasures is reflected in the Tofoke[1] name for the missionary:

mondele bosongo go liande	the generic name for the white man; literally, the white man from the river
bo lokasa lolikuku likatangama	of the leaf (i.e. book) of *likuku* which is to be read

The reading primer of the Yakusu Mission is entitled *Likuku la Wembe* because its first story after the initial syllable drill concerns three biting flies, *likuku* and *wembe* and *ʃɔi*. The name of the book is here reproduced in the drum language. I know of no other case (except the reference to the Bible in the Kele drum language) where European printed matter is given publicity on an African talking drum! The name for the State officer on this Tofoke drum represents him as powerful as the most formidable animal in the Central African forest:

bondele bosongo ko liande	the white man from the river
bo ofulufulu waluwa mbele	the giant leopard, destroyer of houses

The Olombo tribe to the west of Lokele-land seem to be interested in the ability of the white missionary to teach writing rather than reading. Their name for him is:

bosongo bolemba bokake mbula	white man evil spirit as bad as rain (generic name)
bo lokasa lobasongo lokasɔnɛlɛ	of the leaf (paper) which can be written on

---

[1] The Tofoke or Esɔ people are an inland forest tribe reached from the river by the first white men.

CHAPTER VII

BIRTHS, MARRIAGES AND DEATHS

BEFORE going on to describe full drum messages relating to the life of the tribe it is necessary to mention several points which must be remembered in connection with all messages beaten out.

First of all, there is usually an opening signal or alert. In the Kele drum language this usually consists of several repetitions of high note — low note, high note — low note, represented in speech by the drummers themselves as *ki kɛ, ki kɛ.*

The Olombo villagers near Yakusu begin with a roll on the high note of the drum consisting of about twenty taps rapidly succeeding one another. In the baMbɔlɛ villages, as explained on page 27, there are men who announce their drum messages in a characteristic way because they have positions of authority in the villages in which they live. After the initial call-signal comes the name of the person to whom the message is to be sent. Then comes the business of the message. This will be repeated three or four times, often more if the message is a long one, and the name of the person to whom it is sent will also be repeated. Finally, when the drummer feels sure that the message has 'gone through', he may add the name of the person who has requested the message to be sent (e.g. the village chief) and then he concludes with a series of low notes, sometimes terminated with a little flourish on both notes of the drum to characterize his own particular beating — a kind of signature tune. These various parts are frequently punctuated by beats consisting of the two drum notes beaten simultaneously — a sound rendered in speech by the drummer as *kbɛi, kbɛi*; as they are beaten out it is clear that the drummer is collecting his thoughts and deciding what he shall beat out next in his message.

Obviously the opening and closing signals, together with the many repetitions needed, all go to make the drum message a rather lengthy affair. Messages lasting twenty minutes are commonly heard at Yakusu, and many messages are even longer, although it is clear that in these the drummer is enjoying himself in sending out his news about a recent or forthcoming event rather than concerning himself in reaching the people for whom the message is intended. Even without the repetitions required for 'sending home' the message, the necessary use of stereotyped phrases instead of single words means that the drum message is much longer than the corresponding spoken message. Compare, for instance, this spoken message and the words necessary to put the same message into the drum language:

English: The missionary is coming up-river to our village to-morrow. Bring water and firewood to his house.

Kele (spoken): *bosongo atoya ko nda bokenge wasu lɛlɛngɔ. eʃaka balia la toala ko nda ndakɔ yande.*

Kele (drummed):

bosongo olimo ko nda lokonda	white man spirit from the forest
wa lokasa lwa lonjwa	of the leaf used for roofs
atoya likolo atoya likolo	comes up-river, comes up-river
ko lɛlɛngcekaliekele	when to-morrow has risen
likolo ko nda use	on high in the sky
ko nda likelenge liboki	to the town and the village
liaaka la iso	of us
yaku yaku yaku yaku	come, come, come, come
yatikeke balia ba lɔkɔila	bring water of *lɔkɔila* vine
yatikeke tokolokolo twa toala	bring sticks of firewood
ko nda ndakɔya tumbe elundu likolo	to the house with shingles high up above
ya bosongo olimo ko nda lokonda	of the white man spirit from the forest
wa lokasa lwa lonjwa	of the leaf used for roofs

Drummed out with the necessary opening and closing signals, the names of addressees and addressor and all the repetitions needed to make sure that the tasks expected would be adequately performed, this message could easily take up ten minutes of a drummer's time.

Births. News of the birth of a child is not often drummed out and some tribes do not seem to have special sentences connected with such an event. But it does form the subject of drum language when the birth has taken place while the father is away on a journey or out fishing on the river and can be recalled to the town. The message used by the Lokele people is of interest in that it refers to the custom of the confinement of the expectant mother in a small hut at the back of the main living quarters before and during the birth of the baby. Here it is:

the wife of so-and-so
who has been living in the little house in the court-yard
has given birth to a child, a boy (or girl)
set down the knot that is in your heart (cf. p. 39)
throw away the knot of the heart up into the air

According to Father Hulstaert, who investigated the drum language of the Nkundo people, the announcement of the birth of a child gives more anatomical details than that of the Lokele folk:

the mats have been spread out
a man (one who holds fast lance and shield)
or a woman (friendship of a woman)
has come on a journey from the womb
and is born to so-and-so

The Yaamba birth announcement (Yaamba is the north-eastern section of the baMbɔlɛ territory) is:

set the heart down (= don't worry)
the child has not set down his feet (= the child has not remained behind)
in the black body of the mother

But while some tribes do not seem to possess a special call for the birth of a child, most tribes have an announcement on the drum for the birth of twins. 'Hello twins' on the Lokele talking drum is:

ho baasa kelele ho baasa kelele	ho twins, *kelele* (a greeting word)
bolunda kelele baasa kelele	poison ordeal, ho twins
bokɛsɛ bileme ya wɛngɔ nda liande koolaka yafele la yamboku	if you throw your old bit of a net into the river you will catch fish
wike wike	many many

This last metaphor of the riverine Lokele people is quite humorous! But the reference to *bolunda* invites our attention. It is well known that in some African communities twins are looked upon as omens of the wrath of the spirit world and, according to ancient traditions, should be killed at birth. But this attitude is not to be observed in the tribes inhabiting the Stanleyville area of Belgian

Congo. Indeed, twins are welcomed as a valuable addition to the family. It is difficult therefore to account for the reference to the poison used for the ordeal. Possibly in former generations some ceremony involving infusions of the bark of the *bolunda* tree was necessary for those who had borne twins but, while the memory of this has been perpetuated in the conservative drum language, it has been lost from the living memory of the tribe for no drummers have been able to give me a reason for the inclusion of this word *bolunda* in the message greeting twins. It is interesting to find that in his account of the Tumba drum language an American missionary, the Rev. R. T. Clarke, gives the Tumba drum greetings for twins as: *ocobico ocobico* and adds that this cannot be translated and is possibly archaic.

Marriages. In Central Africa marriage is by no means the romantic affair to which we European peoples are accustomed. It is rather in the nature of a contract between the families of the boy and girl about to be married. Boys whom I have expected to leave school and get married before settling down to work in the village or in a large town sometimes come back to Yakusu at the beginning of a new school year and inform me that they will be with us for a further period of scholastic training because, contrary to their expectations, the family had not been able to get together sufficient wealth for providing the boy with a wife. The boy is usually quite ignorant of the name or village of the girl who will be his future helpmate, but is content to leave the choice in the hands of his father and the rest of the family when the necessary bride-price becomes available. So we cannot write of a drum message which corresponds with European wedding bells.

Let it not be thought, however, that 'love's young dream' is unknown in Central Africa. Far from it! When once a fiancée has been chosen for a young man, he may use the drum as a means of letting his betrothed know the intensity of his feelings for her. This drum correspondence does not have the privacy which we ourselves would desire for such communications. Mεnεokenge of Yasendo (*see* page 44) told me that in his tribe the young swain would first take a magical preparation[1] of a certain forest tree and rub this on the drumsticks. Then he would

---

[1] Love-charms are quite an important part of the Central African Pharmacopoeia. One fairly common forest bush is rubbed on the teeth, for instance, to give the lover's words irresistibly persuasive powers. 'No girl could refuse a man who has rubbed his teeth with these leaves', say our Yakusu men.

beat out the name of his young lady friend (as the daughter of such-and-such a man) and follow up with:

botema falifalifalifali   my heart beats pit-a-pat, pit-a-pat

There is probably more in this message but Mɛnɛokenge was reticent in giving me further details.

Should marriage arrangements proceed according to the traditional plan, then the drum would be used in calling together the girl's family for the final settlement of goods and money to be handed over to them by the boy's family before the girl could be allowed to leave her home. A message of this sort would be sent, for instance, in the baMbɔlɛ area:

(so-and-so)
come in the morning
let us sit down together
let us look into the palaver
let us look into the affair
of my daughter
who is to take the journey of a wife to-morrow.

The only drum message which resembles the pealing of wedding bells in Central Africa is that used for an irregular marriage when a great deal of excitement is aroused and maintained in the community by the talking drum. These drum calls are getting more and more frequent in Lokele villages as traditional modes of behaviour are breaking down under the disruptive influence of white civilization. Sometimes owing to the grasping nature of a girl's parents who demand more and more money or goods from the boy's family before allowing their daughter to become a wife, and also owing to the impetuosity of the young people themselves, the girl will run away from her father's village or be carried thence by her lover. The pair make for the village of the future husband. When they arrive, there is great rejoicing, for the clan to which the husband belongs has, in a measure, scored over the clan of the girl. The members have obtained their 'purchase' before completing all the money transactions and now the irate parents of the girl will be obliged to follow her up and wait for the final instalment of the marriage price. The drum joins in the crowd's rejoicing by beating out:

lisalakutu kolongela ku ku ku kukulokele   the owl has overcome
                                              hu hu huu

I have not been able to discover what connection the owl has with this part of traditional Lokele behaviour; further investigations are necessary. Then the drum announces the name of the clan and village from which the girl has come and finally incites the crowd to further noise by drumming:

toliole mbu tu tu   shall we open eh? eh? eh?

probably referring to opening up the town to allow the parents of the girl to come in and claim the completion of the bridal price payments. When the community hears that drum question they shout back in chorus with the drum:

tolioleke o   don't let us open oh!

To hear the acclamation with which this shout is made leaves no doubt about the triumphant nature of the *démarche* made by the boy's people.

Deaths. There is no mistaking the death drum of the various Central African tribes. It is begun on the Lokele drum by a special signal of 'alert' in place of the *ki kɛ* we described above. This signal is:

walelaka (repeated thrice)   you will cry

followed by:

bileli ko nda baiso   tears in the eyes
bolelo ko nda bɔnɔkɔ   wailing in the mouth

Then follows the name of the person who has died and his village. The drum explains what has happened by using the expression we have already described on page 37 (corpse) and finishes off by a repetition of the alert: *walelaka*. Sometimes the idea that the spirit has left the body is expressed in the message, thus:

asoosilela bolio wa olimo ko   he has finished in the corpse of
nda lokonda   the spirit of the forest

For a death in war the drum reminds listeners of the arms the man carried:

asoosilela bolio wa ita wa   he has finished in the body of
yeto ya likonga   war of the metal of the spear
la likuka la botukola   and the shield

If an important personage has died the drum may honour his memory by adding, at the beginning and end of the message, the words:

tolakondeloko tolaoteloko 'I never seen the like since I was born'
(which is the best rendering of the words)

This ending is also used when announcing something of grave import.

In some parts of West Africa it is believed that drum messages are not frustrated by the death of the person concerned but that the drum can serve as a means of communicating with the spirit world. A custom of this kind prevails on the signal drums of some South American Indians (who use a code rather than a drum language, however). The Jibaro Indians of Ecuador and Peru summon the spirits to partake of the ceremonial feasts of narcotics or manioc and palm fruits by special rhythmic messages on their 'tundu' slit-drum. They believe that the slit-drum is itself a representation of the spirit which appears as the anaconda or great water-snake. That the spiritual world can appreciate messages sent by the drum is clearly the belief of the drummer of the Ewe tribe described by Westermann. He writes (34. s. 9):

> As a rule conversations by means of the drum language begin with an invocation (also drummed) or an act of praise to God; but here is used always the name of the supreme Deity, never of a lower deity. Such invocations are:
>
> Great God, Creator of the Heaven and Earth, who
> givest rain and sunshine, of whom we are not afraid.
> Great God help us;
> when Thou helpest us we are not afraid.
> Great God help us;
> when Thou helpest us we are not afraid.
>
> The roads cross the rivers,
> the rivers cross the roads.
> Which are the older in time?
> The roads proceed from Man but the rivers come from God.
>
> The termite eats through things;
> she eats through God's things;
> but the termite does not eat God Himself.[1]

[1] These drum messages show us that belief in the spirit world and in the spiritual realities of life is part of the heritage of the African. This does not necessarily mean that he is Christian, however. The Christian missionary does not have to convince Africans of the reality of God the Creator and Sustainer of the World, but he does have to try to graft the Christian belief of God the Father on to the spiritual background which is reflected in the drum language messages we have described here.

CHAPTER VIII

SPORTING EVENTS

'HUNTIN', fishin', and shootin' ' are occupations which are well known to most African tribesmen and in which they are well skilled. They form an essential part of everyday life and are by no means the prerogatives of a leisured class. Because they take up a good deal of the villager's time they are well represented in the drum language.

To call friends to assist in hunting, a Yaamba man will beat out:

to-day has dawned
let us go a journey into the forest
with the net of the forest of trees and
mboloko and *fambi*

Mboloko and *fambi* are two forms, one small and the other large, of the forest antelope. We note here their drum names because they recur in the drum languages of other Central African tribes. For instance, the Nkundo tribe, as reported by Hulstaert (28), and van Goethem (27), drum out this message during the evening before the departure of a hunting expedition:

when morning has come
the net on the shoulder, staff in hand
let us go into the forest
let us go hunting with sticks (on which to hang the net)
mbambi la *mboloko* la *mbuli*
look out for a good place

Note again the reference to these forest animals; *mbuli* is yet another form of antelope. The neighbouring Tumba tribe explains clearly the motive which urges an African to his 'huntin' ' It is, notice, quite a different one from that which keeps European hunting parties keen on their sport.

We have been here since long ago
men with nets on shoulders and knives at sides
we want meat which is in the forest
where live *mpambi* la *mboloko*
we don't want to stay at home to-day
our bellies are dying of hunger, they are empty

But net and staves are not the only requirements of the hunter in Central Africa. He needs a small dog which will drive the hunted animal into the net. This dog is also called up on the drum when a man wishes to set off into the forest to look for meat. The hunter will send this message to the owner of the dog in the baMbɔlɛ forest:

giant (a term of respect) dog,
son which says *kweekwee*
we are going, we are going,
those of you men who are going with the net
don't stay behind

The word *kweekwee* is really an onomatopoeic representation of the noise the dog makes when barking. Compare it with similar representation of the voice in the name for a fowl (p. 33).

While these calls to the hunt are used by the forest dwellers, the riverine people like the Lokele tribe send out invitations to join in fishing parties. These are not so large in numbers as the hunting parties but are usually arranged by individuals who own canoes and nets, members of the family being called to assist during the fishing period. The leader of the party would call up his friends by name and tell them of his proposals by some such message as the following:

come, come, come, come,
with the bits of nets
into the canoe which floats
let us go together
on the river

The expeditions described above with their attendant drum calls are really the occupations of the peoples rather than pastimes. But the drum is useful also in regulating the leisure of the people as well as its labour. It serves, for instance, to announce that universal African pastime: the dance. And when the fun has commenced the drum will be in constant use to stimulate the participants. The dance is usually announced the evening before it is to take place and then again in the morning. The phrases used by the Lokele folk have already been given in connection with the drum name devised for the writer, namely:

all of you, all of you
come, come, come, come,

let us dance
in the evening
when the sky has gone down river
down to the ground[1]

The language of the Tumba tribe is perhaps more expressive:

(name of village called to the dance)
strengthen yourselves
we don't want meetings with mats and beds
we want gatherings for dancing
men, women and children, we have all gone
we left long ago; mats and beds remain behind.

I have seen a village dancing team obey the call to join in the dance of a neighbouring community (in this case the dance was held in connection with the coming-of-age of a group of village boys). As the group of young dancers approached the village square they broke into a run, keeping perfect time, their lithe, athletic limbs shining with the oil rubbed into the skin and their feather head-dresses bobbing up and down to their movements. I was forcibly reminded of the movements (but less agile) of a European football team leaving the dressing-rooms and taking the field.

The slit-drum is used to beat out the dance rhythm, although the principal part in the dance orchestra is taken by the skin-topped drum, *ngɔma*, and sometimes the wedge-shaped slit-drum, *longombe*. When the slit-drum helps to beat out the dance rhythm it does not 'talk' as for drum messages. A Nigerian writer, Delano, describing his own tribal customs (14), says that:

when an ordinary dance is performed the drummer's task . . . is important for he speaks by means of the drum to every dancer and the best listeners are always the best dancers.

But no Lokele drummer will agree that there is anything more in the slit-drum's dance-beats than mere rhythm. It is still true for the Lokele people that the best listeners are the best dancers, for the dancer must listen to the changes in rhythm in order to make the necessary changes in the footwork of the dance; but the slit-drum abandons its 'talking' function during the dancing.

Wrestling. One institution which serves as a pastime, especially

[1] For the Kele words *see* pp. 44 and 45.

at certain seasons of the year, is still called 'dancing' by the Lokele folk. This sport is not traditionally a Lokele institution but was borrowed from the baEna people at Stanley Falls, as the drum name for the 'dance' shows.[1] The talking drum plays an all-important part in this practice. First of all comes the message to the villagers announcing the event. This message is usually sent the evening before the wrestling is to take place. In place of the usual alert of *ki kɛ*, there is a special code phrase:

kbɛi kbɛi kitakita kiki	(which has no verbal base; see p. 53 for the meaning of *kbɛi*)

Then:

la bolongo lolikalika	the dance
lokasekwele ko nda liande	which has come from the river
lya bainatende la ſanga	of the baEna folk with fish-traps
ſa ilonga	

These messages would be repeated again and again with invitations to the populace to join in at the appointed time. If the match were to be between the members of the village called and men of a neighbouring village, then the name of this latter would be given in the announcement. At the time of the wrestling match the crowd gathers together to form a ring, the two opposing groups (village sections, or villages) facing one another. One or more slit-drums are placed on the ground and their drummers stand ready. Usually each opposing group provides a set of drummers who take turns to beat out the messages used; the beating is almost continuous during the match. Two drummers may beat on one drum, one using the proper rubber-covered drumsticks and the other armed with small, thin sticks which, while not injuring the drum lips, give a pleasing accompaniment to the main message. After much delay (the European onlooker almost invariably dubs this African wrestling as very slow and grows impatient) one man decides to step into the ring and challenge the opposing side with a demand for an opponent. The drum heralds him with:

efefe eloaloa efefe eloaloa	the hero, full of pride

He walks round the ring seemingly unconcerned while the

---

[1] The baEna, on the other hand, regard ordinary dancing as coming to them from the Lokele people.

opponents eye him and measure themselves up with him.[1] One man may then step out and throw down in front of the 'hero' a small piece of grass or leaf. This is the sign that the challenge is accepted. They both look round for lengths of rope which are handed to them by the crowd, each man receiving his piece from his own supporters. The drum expectantly works up excitement with the message:

> *liango likwesane liango likwesane*   let the wrestling begin
> *takanaka tolinge takanaka tolinge*   trip one another up

The rope is tied firmly around the waist of each man and then they bend towards one another, each man placing one shoulder beneath the opposite shoulder of his opponent. In this arched position they grasp the rope belts behind the back and begin to prance round the ring with legs outstretched. The drum keeps up its jeering call: 'Trip him up! Trip him up!' and the crowd looks on expectantly. Often it takes several minutes before anything more happens because each man is awaiting his opportunity of making a quick jerk to get his opponent off his feet. The drummer may begin to get tired with the waiting and his customary beating degenerates into mere rhythmic dance-like beating. Instead of the message we have given above we hear fragments such as:

> lia . . . li . . . sane, lia . . . li . . . sane
> takanaka to . . . nge, takanaka to . . . nge

But suddenly a leg shoots out and curls round its opposite number; a quick heave and the opponent is off the ground, swung round to the side and landed on the back squarely. It is a throw! The crowd supporting the winner yells with delight while the drum exuberantly announces the success to all the world by a prolonged roll on the low note of the drum . . . kbuuuuuuuuuuuuuu! The thrown man walks back to his little group disconsolately while the winner remains behind in the ring as the drum praises him with its message:

> *efefe eloaloa efefe eloaloa*   see the hero! full of pride!

[1] No bout could take place unless the opponents were of equal size, height and weight. What the Englishman calls pluckiness in a young lad challenging an older opponent is, to the African, sheer nonsense and not to be allowed: 'He's not my size, therefore I do not fight him.' David in fighting Goliath breaks all rules of Central African wrestling associations, and the repressive, restraining words of King Saul and the 'older brothers' represent traditional African behaviour.

Olombo children learning to drum on bamboo models
of slit-drum, Yakusu

A Yafɔlɔ drum-maker at work

If the man is a wrestling 'star' some of his younger supporters may give him special publicity by dancing round the ring and jumping towards him with arms outstretched vertically as much as to say to the opposing side: 'This is his height! Can't you find anyone like him to challenge him?' They accompany their antics with yells and shrieks.

It is interesting to read an account of a wrestling match in West Africa which was written by Mungo Park towards the end of the eighteenth century. He writes:

> It must not be unobserved that the combatants were animated by the music of a drum, by which their actions were in some measure regulated.

Clearly, Mungo Park was witnessing a wrestling match very similar to that of the Lokele people.

War. In the days before white occupation or Arab domination, war was almost considered in the nature of a sport. A conflict of the nature of European war is entirely unknown in Central Africa and cannot even now be understood by tribesmen there. If hostilities lasted more than a few weeks it was time to parley and seek peace by mutual agreement rather than risk destruction of too much material and too many lives.[1] The drum would not be used normally to announce the gathering together of an expedition for war. This would be foolish in giving publicity to what is essentially a secret move. But it did find its voice in announcing the arrival of the enemy in the town and in calling together the warriors. In Kele drum language this call was a special alert consisting of two low notes followed by two high notes, or in some cases, a repetition of the word *ito*, meaning 'look out'. Then:

> war which watches for opportunities
> has come to the town
> belonging to us
> to-day as it has dawned
> come, come, come, come

[1] This outlook is clearly reflected in the story, reported by a missionary at the beginning of the 1914-18 war. One Lokele chief, unable to comprehend the continuance of hostilities after a few weeks had gone by, said to the missionary: 'Listen to what your people must do in order to stop this fighting. Let the Chief of England send five handsome maidens to the Chief of Germany and the conflict would end immediately. That is our way of arranging matters of this kind.'

Interestingly enough, this special alert has remained in these days when it is no longer needed for its primary purpose (thanks to government). It is the call on the Mission Station drum for men to go back to their work after the midday rest or early in the morning. A missionary employer of labour cannot help wondering sometimes what would have become of a Lokele village in the olden days if its inhabitants obeyed the call to war with as great reluctance as their children to-day obey the call to work!

Hulstaert gives a Nkundo drum call to war which would be used for calling up help from a neighbouring friendly village:

> *ki ki ki ki ke* (initial signal)
> (name of town called)
> come along here
> mats are outstretched (for wounded?)
> *ki ki ki ki ke*

while the Tumba war drum tries to stimulate the prowess and courage of the villagers who are being attacked:

> *ki ki ki ki ki ki*
> make the drum strong
> strengthen your legs, spear, shaft and head
> the noise of running feet; think not to run away

Initiation ceremonies. Not exactly of the nature of sporting events, but yet definite institutions of the tribe, holding the interest of the people at certain special times, are the secret ceremonies and initiation rites common to a number of African communities. We could include the circumcision ceremonies too, which may be carried out during the initiation rites (as in the Kabile ceremonies of the Mbae people) or separated from them in time (as for the Lokele people).

Circumcision is usually practised on young boys before puberty. If a man dies before his sons reach this age and they are nearing it, then the custom is to perform the operation as soon after the death of the father as possible. But in the normal course of events the father himself makes arrangements for the circumcision of his sons and perhaps the sons of relatives in the same clan. A few men in the district are recognized as competent surgeons for the operation; they may, or may not, be identical with the *kanga* or witch-doctor. One of these men is asked by the father of the boys

66

to come to his home and operate on a given day. The drum language serves to remind him and others of the appointed time:

> *kbɛi kbɛtɛkbɛtɛ* (a special alert for circumcision)
> let us cut the foreskin
> the heart will be pulled (a reference to the pain)
> to-morrow when it has risen in the sky
> the male is wounded as in war
> the male recovers
> remains only the corpse of the male

This latter phrase is said, by Lokele drummers, to refer to the possibility of death from the wound — a possibility that was not infrequently an occurrence owing to infection and ignorance of proper methods of dealing with dirty wounds.

That the calling of the surgeon is an individual rather than a tribal or even a village affair is shown by the personal nature of the message of the Yasendo drum:

> (name of the surgeon)
> come, come on a journey in the morning
> come and put
> the metal of the knife
> to the foreskin of my son

The drum message from a further baMbɔlɛ group (Botunga) shows that no attempt is made to encourage the youngsters by saying: 'Never mind, it won't hurt!' To all and sundry in the village it announces:

> *kbɛi*, the foreskin-o!
> father and mother
> let us cut the foreskin
> weeping bitterly in the heart

The secret ceremony rites, called *libeli*, practised by the Lokele in past generations (*libeli* is now practically extinct on the river although carried on sporadically in the forest area by the baMbɔlɛ) are most certainly a foreign institution borrowed from peoples living to the east or north-east. This extraneous origin of the rites explains the fact that the talking drum[1] plays no part in the rites themselves, serving only to call up the sponsors or

---

[1] A Lokele institution from time immemorial.

'mothers' of the boys to be initiated. For these sponsors the drum message is:

> *kɛ kɛ ki kɛ* (a special alert for the *libeli* rites)
> elders of the forest
> come here

The rites were performed in a sacred grove of trees found at the end of a Lokele village — hence the reference to the forest in this call. The initiates themselves were given the name of:

> *ngele yaambɔlu bɔndɔbɔndɔ*

the significance of which I have been unable to determine; Lokele drummers questioned about the words say that the whole phrase is simply a name handed down to them but they cannot translate it into spoken Lokele. This fact again emphasizes the 'foreign' nature of the *libeli* rites.

The establishment of the extraneous origin of rites such as the *libeli* of the Lokele people and the *kabile* of the Mbae tribe has more than an academic interest. The Christian Church which has arisen in the Yakusu area opposed the initiation ceremonies because of their deceitful nature and the immoral practices associated with them. In some quarters the missionaries directing the Church in this area have been criticized for not attempting to retain an 'essential tribal culture element' or for destroying a part of the African's heritage. It is true to say, however, that the *libeli* ceremonies of the Lokele people are as foreign to Lokele-land as Arabic dress or European writing symbols. The writer was able to use this argument with native people in the Mbae area during a recent recrudescence of *kabile* in some riverine villages. Certain groups of Europeans in the district were quoted as wishing these ceremonies well on the grounds that it was good to foster the traditional behaviour of the tribe. But Mbae men agreed that the *kabile* rites were not a part of ancient Mbae tribal behaviour but had come from the East in fairly recent times. Their perpetuation or abolition therefore rests on their value to tribal life at the present day; and Christian leaders of the tribe recognize the ceremonies as harmful and anti-social.

CHAPTER IX

POTPOURRI

THERE are a number of drum messages and methods of beating them out which have not been described in earlier chapters. It is convenient to group them together now, although they do not belong to any one set of Central African customs or events.

When a Lokele drummer has a lengthy announcement to make which does not require immediate action on the part of the audience, e.g. when he is announcing something for the morrow, he often adopts a very distinctive form of beating which consists in dividing up his 'news' into short items and drumming these items out one by one, separating each by a long invitation to come along to the appointed meeting place. This invitation is the usual word for 'come', namely *yaku*, but it is beaten very slowly, like this:

ya . . . ku . . . ya . . . ku . . . ya . . . ku . . . ya . . . ku, and so on.
 L H L H L H L H

Here is a message of this kind telling the people to meet together on the morrow because the Government officer will be arriving in the village to collect taxes:

ki kɛ, ki kɛ, ki kɛ, ki kɛ (initial alert)
all of you, all of you, all of you,
ya . . . ku . . . ya . . . ku . . . ya . . . ku . . .
let us gather together at the house of the white man
ya . . . ku, etc.
when to-morrow has risen in the sky
ya . . . ku, etc.
bring along the money which arranges matters
ya . . . ku, etc.
to the house of the white man
ya . . . ku, etc.
he has been to the villages down-river
ya . . . ku, etc.
now he comes to our own town
ya . . . ku, etc.
you fishermen on the river
ya . . . ku, etc.

bring your feet back, bring your legs back
ya . . . ku, etc.
to our own town
ya . . . ku, etc.

and so on for many repetitions of his news, until the message may last for a whole hour or more.

Another interesting form of beating which is not often heard but cannot be mistaken when it occurs is that of 'dictation beating'. The chief may not wish to leave his house in order to request that a message be sent to his people; or he may be anxious to send over just the right kind of words and, if he relied on another drummer, these might not be forthcoming. So he sits down at his own small drum, usually on the veranda of his house, and beats away to the special drummer stationed by the side of one of the big town drums overlooking the river. The chief beats out his message on the shrill-timbred small drum. As he finishes his phrase, the deep-throated village drum takes it up and beats it out. The alternation of the same phrases on the high-toned drum of the chief and immediately afterwards on the low-toned drum overlooking the river is most characteristic.

Clearly the drum language was an institution designed to be used in an African society unaffected by European civilization. Can it adapt itself to the new needs introduced by the white man? We have seen already that the drum can distinguish among the various kinds of white men working in its area, who are given characteristic names which may be full of meaning for the foreigner delving into their significance. And in other ways too, the drum language is shown to be very adaptable. One could say that the river-steamer is a typical product of the white man's presence in Africa. On the drum it has a name which, in Kele, is:

the canoe, very large (like an elephant) of the white man.

So far as I know, the Lokele drummers have not yet devised a name for the aeroplane, but doubtless, when they do so, it will refer to the bird, very large, like an eagle, of the white man.

In chapter VII we mentioned that, although the African is not usually an atheist, yet his theological notions are certainly not Christian and the missionary has a big task in bringing home to him the truth of the Fatherhood of God. Allegations that the African does not really understand the Christian faith are, of

70

course, often read in non-Christian literature about the continent. And many Christian missionaries grow disheartened at times with the difficulties of their job and the apparent slowness with which the implications of the Fatherhood of God are carried out in the everyday lives of African church members. To such antagonists and pessimists the drum name for God as evolved by the Lokele drummers will be of interest. Again we have the adaptation of the drum to a new need — that of God the Father as distinct from God the Creator. The name as drummed out is:

liuwe liSango likasekwele likolo ko nda use
the Father who came down from above

(The word *liuwe*, before *sango* — Father — in the name is a term of respect.) This name is certainly not European in origin, for drum names were not learned in early European controlled schools. It is a spontaneous production of African church members taught on the Mission and it surely contains a germ of Christian belief about God.

Investigations into the meaning of these African drum language phrases often lead to the discovery of some tribal custom or belief hitherto unsuspected. Lokele boys and girls have a custom of welcoming the new moon when it first appears after sunset in the western sky. To a European newly arrived in the village this custom is quite startling for, in the quiet of the evening, there is suddenly a big shout from people standing ·near the house and this cry is taken up on all sides . . . *tandole!* (crescent moon). The drum seems to have no part in this cry of welcome, but I wondered if neighbouring peoples might perhaps use the drum or another instrument on which to send out some kind of message at the new moon's arrival. In course of such questions to Mbae men I received a negative answer about the shout at the time of the new moon, but was given information about the role played by the drum in recalling people from the forest at such a time or informing them of the arrival of the new moon. It was explained to me that villagers at work in the forest, felling trees or making traps and resident in the forest during their work could not gauge properly the rising times of the moon owing to the tree belt screening the horizon. Therefore the drum had to tell them of the imminence of the new moon date, because any work done on the day when the old moon has 'died' and the new moon has not yet appeared, would be liable to bring serious consequences on the man doing it. In all sincerity I was told that a man going to till his garden on that day would most probably be injured by a falling branch. Traps and nets set to catch animals and fish on that day would be quite useless. No work must be done on the day when the moon is hidden. Later questions to other tribesmen show that beliefs of this kind are comparatively widespread among the tribes of the Stanleyville area.

One example has been given (*see* p. 58) of the way in which the drum plays a kind of concerto accompanied by the singing or shouting of the assembled tribesmen. Other examples of this occur. Sometimes a mischievous youth will vary the call of the station drum to release workmen from their labours and will beat out a rhythm represented in speech as:

kɛkɛlɛ kɛkɛlɛ ki kɛ ki . . .

which has no language basis for the Lokele drummer, but may probably be a phrase borrowed from the drum language of another tribe. As soon as this message is heard, everyone yells as hard as he can so that the whole village is in an uproar.

Another case of such a drum concerto is said to be found in the removal of epidemic disease by consigning it to the river current which shall take the malady down-river away from the village. I have never seen this done, but I am told that the medicine-man, *kanga*, would make a special preparation of forest leaves and other magical ingredients which would be thrown into the river in front of the assembled population. As the people shout:

loo kɛndɛ mbole   disease go down-river!

the drum, beaten by a drummer who has smeared himself with the preparation made by the *kanga*, would accompany the crowd with the tonal melody of the phrase used. A drum concerto that actually took place recently in Yakusu was concerned with the expulsion of a woman of bad repute who had created much indignation by her presence in the town. One night they assembled to insult her as she left by canoe and the drum incited the crowd to insults which are best not translated here, the words used having an intimate connection with the behaviour of the woman expelled.

The drum is thus not only the transmitter of information; it is also the entertainer of the people. It can draw a shout and even a laugh from its audience. Crawford in his book, *Back to the Long Grass* (2), referring to the talking drum *mondo* of the south-eastern Congo, writes:

> not a dull, senseless rub-a-dub, but a drum with a tongue wagging out even gossip; a drum that, provided you do not crack it can actually crack a joke. Again and again, across some miles . . . you can hear from a group of silent negroes a burst of laughter . . . they are laughing at the pleasant wit of Mr. *Mondo* five miles off.

Gossip and joke — yes, and curse too! Many a bitter war of past generations in Lokele country has been begun by abuse and cursing from the talking drum. Abuse on the drum is particularly virulent because everyone in the neighbourhood can hear what is said and can join in the laugh against the person victimized. Strangely enough, the abuse which is most commonly used seems to us to be very mild but is seriously insulting to the African. The drum simply calls attention to the head of the person to be ostracized and describes it as a lump! Thus:

> Tom, Dick or Harry,
> listen to the word of the drum
> lump of a head! lump of a head!

To which the indignant Tom, Dick or Harry will reply by announcing to the village in general that this insult is quite undeserved and that he, Tom, Dick or Harry, has not done any wrong to anyone. Thus:

> by the heavens above
> I haven't persecuted any man
> hear the evil word and the evil affair
> which is spoken on the drum
> up to heaven and down to earth   (a reference to the wide-
> sending the drum up to the sky   spreading of the news?)
> with an evil word and an evil affair
> about the body
> ho! how evil is the word and the affair

But doubtless this Tom, Dick or Harry would soon be sending back the very message which he says had insulted him; he might go one further and use the words which we referred to but did not print on page 72. And the probable outcome of these exchanges of abusive drum language would be a fight.

CHAPTER X

HORNS, WHISTLES AND GUITARS

For if the trumpet give an uncertain sound,
Who shall prepare himself to the battle?
ST. PAUL, I Corinthians xiv, v. 8

ALTHOUGH the statement sounds rather 'Irish' it is true to say that the drums are not the only instruments on which the drum language can be transmitted. Were it not for the fact that the African method of communicating at a distance has usually been associated with the talking drum in the minds of European explorers and their readers it would be better to call the language we have been describing a 'signal language' and not specify the instrument used.

The human voice is an instrument at the disposal of all. It is this instrument which is used in ordinary spoken language in order to differentiate meaning by changes in vowels and consonants spoken in various pitches and with differing stresses. But the human voice can also be used to transmit the special drum language where tonal changes are the most important characteristic for determining meaning. For using the voice in this way, Lokele people shout *ki* (or *li* and *ti*) for the high note and *kɛ* (or *lɛ* and *tɛ*) for the low note of the drum language. Different combinations of tones which are required to transmit a drum phrase are thus represented by different combinations of shouted *ki* and *ke*. The name for the white man in this shouted language is, for example:

kɛlɛkɛ kɛliki kɛlikɛlɛkɛ.

Substitute for *kɛ* and *lɛ* the low note and for *ki* and *li* the high note and the tonal pattern of the white man's drum name as given on page 49 is found. These shouted signals are often used by Lokele tribesmen when at work fishing on the river in order to communicate over great distances between their canoes. The tonal patterns conveyed by this method are distinguishable and hence meaningful where the distance makes it impossible to distinguish between the vowels and consonants necessary for correct understanding of ordinary spoken words. The shouting-at-a-distance language described here for the Lokele people is common in many other tribes of Central Africa. The actual syllables used to represent the high and low tones may vary; Mbae men use *cu* and *cɔ* while baNgombe drummers refer to *gu* and *gɔ*.

The spoken signals of the shouting-at-a-distance language are used by drummers to explain their drum language phrases to the uninitiated. Anyone hearing the pattern:

kiti kɛtikɛlɛ kɛtɛ

would be excused if he found it difficult to connect the sounds given to him with the word for moon in spoken Kele. But compare this phrase with the drum name for moon given on page 33 and make the substitutions as described above. It is clear that the tonal pattern is adequately given by the *ki* and *kɛ* notation shown here.

One very prominent student of African languages tried to get to the bottom of the drum language employed in West Africa at the end of the nineteenth century and was given what is clearly the shouting-at-a-distance signals for the phrases used as names on the drum. He transcribed them carefully and then compared them with the spoken words for the corresponding objects. Thus he wrote:

dog drum language: *kuku totokulo*; spoken: *mbo*
water drum language: *togolo golo golo golo*; spoken: *madiba*

and he drew the conclusion: 'These signals have not the slightest resemblance with the spoken language.' This conclusion has probably served to deepen the mystery which some people have felt exists around the subject of drum languages in Africa. But what the tribesmen had done in all good faith was to give the investigator the *tonal patterns only* of the phrases drummed out for 'dog' and 'water', representing a high tone by *ku* (probably) and *lu*, and a low tone by *to*, *go* and *lo*. Had they provided the investigator with the words of the drum phrases actually used instead of the tonal patterns of these he would quickly have recognized the connection between drummed and spoken language.

Shouting-at-a-distance is also used by forest tribesmen who make the forest glades echo as they shout out messages from one garden to another. The story is told of a Government official who was anxious to prevent the wholesale dispersal of the village people to the forest before he entered a town to collect taxes or deal with palavers. He realized that the news of his approach was being transmitted from village to village by the talking drum, and so required all drums to be brought to a central village and there impounded. But the villagers were undismayed, for they could still send out exactly the same messages with their shouting-at-a-distance language and their horns, although the effective distances of message transmission were certainly somewhat reduced by the State action.

Another instrument at the disposal of everyone for transmitting signals is the whistle which can be made with the two lips. This is commonly used by the schoolboys at Yakusu who can tell their friends of all the doings of the white schoolmaster by means of this whistled language. It is the African schoolboy's way of shouting 'cave' when the master is on his way to the disorderly form-room. It is also the signal of African workmen, taking a rest on their hoes or at their saws and planes, to tell everyone that the overseer is on the way or that the white man is in the offing. A rapid whistled signal — and everyone is hard at work. Here again the lips whistle out the tonal patterns of the phrases which make up the drum language. A traveller in Nigeria described a similar use of whistling among the Ibo people:

> I myself, have been whistled through a strange town, my passage being announced by one man to another as I passed along the bush path, the signallers remaining out of sight (BASDEN, 13. p. 358).

From whistling with the lips it is a short step to whistling on small tubular instruments. And we find that many tribes use the signal-language on such whistles or flutes. Sometimes the whistles are to be found in a tribe which possesses the talking drum. Thus the youngsters of the farther baMbɔlɛ people make a small whistle out of the spherical fruit of a forest tree which is pierced at three points. One hole serves as a mouth-piece and by opening or closing the others two notes are obtained which give the two tones required to transmit the tonal patterns of the drum phrases. A mission teacher told me that the boys often serenade older relatives by blowing their drum names outside the huts and then expect some kind of gift in exchange. Central African carol singing indeed!

But in other parts of Africa signalling whistles are found where drums are unknown for the purpose of sending messages. A distinguished French linguist and ethnologist, Professor Labouret, describes the whistles from the tribes of the Lobi group in West Africa. After referring to a whistle made from a forest fruit much in the way described above for the baMbɔlɛ people, Labouret says:

> This has been reproduced in wood cut from a piece of the tree which gives the fruit, and a mouth-piece and a tail added . . . The body is elongated so as to give a narrower straighter shape in which can be noted usually two holes, sometimes three and rarely four. . . .
>
> The whistle serves to send certain agreed signals and even to express a language analogous to those drummed out in neighbouring regions. . . .
>
> Each native of the male sex possesses in his village a short refrain known by everyone. In order to correspond one begins by whistling the refrain of the person one is calling and he replies, then the sentence is whistled giving the object of the communication. For example:
>
> ina si gal bi   ina si gal bi   come let us dance[1]
> B A B A   B   B A B   A   B

where A is the high note and B is the low note.

Yet another instrument on which the signal language can be played out is the two-toned horn. This is commonly made from an elephant's tusk or from the horn of another animal such as the buffalo or the large antelope. There are always two holes pierced in horns used for transmitting the signal language; one hole at the tip and the other on the side near the tip of the horn. The horn is blown through the side, and the thumb, by stopping or leaving open the end hole, serves to modulate two notes, these being adequate for sending out the tonal melodies of the phrases making up the signal language.

Finally we must refer to an instrument which uses the same principle as the drum language in rather an unexpected way. This is the lute or guitar; sɛsɛ, made in the Stanleyville region by the Olombo and some other forest peoples. Ethnologists believe that this instrument is not indigenous to Central Africa but came from Madagascar with the Arab traders during their slave raids into the interior. Certainly the bOlombo agree that the Arabs

---

[1] LABOURET, H., *Les tribus du Rameau Lobi*, Paris Records, 1931.

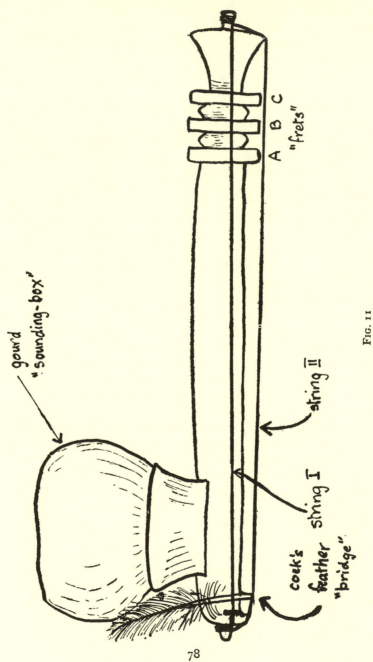

gourd "sounding-box"

A B C "frets"

string II

string I

cock's feather "bridge"

Fig. 11

The Sese of the Bolombo Tribe

brought their *sɛsɛ*; but the Arabs could not have used it in the way we are about to describe because their language is not a tonal one as is the Olombo tongue. Soon after my arrival at Yakusu for the first time I noticed one of these lutes in the hands of a man from a nearby village. I got him to make a copy for me and to come along several times to my house so as to teach me how to play the instrument. During one of these lessons he wished to demonstrate to me a game of 'hide-and-seek' in which, he said, the *sɛsɛ* could take part. He called up to the house several friends who made a ring around him on the veranda. One of them was then instructed to go away out of sight while I was to hide a small coin anywhere within the ring of men. I put a coin inside the pocket of one of them. The *sɛsɛ* then began to play a tune and the young man who had gone some distance away during the hiding of the coin was recalled. He came into the ring and proceeded to look for the coin. Not a word was spoken and I was careful to see that no facial signs were made by the friends in the ring to the man looking for the coin, but as he walked round the ring he stopped in front of the man who held the coin and it was not long before he had it out of the man's pocket. This was repeated again and again and, although at the time I was conscious of some change occurring in the tune of the *sɛsɛ*, I had to admit that I did not know how the trick was done — much to the amusement of my African friends. It was not until several years later that I began to suspect that the two-toned melodies of the drum language were probably the explanation of the game of 'hide-and-seek' with the *sɛsɛ* accompaniment. And when I questioned one of the Mission workmen who possesses a *sɛsɛ*, he agreed that such was the case and told me the actual sentences used to direct the man finding the hidden object. The tonal melodies of these sentences are then worked into the usual *sɛsɛ* tune so that the man who is listening receives clear instructions as to how to find the object. Thus:

if the seeker has overstepped the mark:	*yaku la mbisa* L H L H L come back
if the seeker has not gone far enough:	*omaci ko la felo* L L H L L L L you leave it in front

or: *yaku ko la felo*

L H L L LL

come on in front

if the seeker is on the spot: *olenjeke, olenjeke*

HH H L HH H L

don't forget, don't forget!

and the instrument plays a triumphant little tune when the object is found.

In an account of a voyage to the Kingdom of Kongo, published in 1591, a Portuguese explorer named Duarte Lopez said that the Kongo people possessed a lute. Describing this instrument, the account says:

> More than this (and very wonderful) by means of this instrument they indicate all that other people would express by words of what is passing in their minds and by merely touching the strings signify their thought. (6. page 111.)

Did someone try the *sɛsɛ* trick on Duarte Lopez?

A Kabile initiate of the Mbae tribe

CHAPTER XI

THE FUTURE OF THE DRUM LANGUAGES OF AFRICA

One of the most significant economic changes which is widespread in colonial areas is the decay of indigenous crafts . . . (*Mass Education in Africa*. White Paper; Colonial No. 186.)

ALTHOUGH the drum language is essentially the same as the spoken language, yet, because it consists of stereotyped phrases which represent objects and actions, it takes a serious effort to learn it. There is also a mechanical skill to be acquired, namely, the beating of the tones of the syllables on the two lips of the slit-drum. Hence we find that learning the drummer's art is begun quite early in the life of the prospective drummer. In Lokele-land boys desiring to make themselves proficient in the drum language cut two differently pitched pieces of wood (usually the light, resonant wood of the *botumbe* or 'umbrella' tree) and place these across their knees as they sit on the ground. Then, for hours at a stretch, they will beat away on these sticks with two small clubs. Instead of the *botumbe* sticks they may take a fairly thick bamboo stem and cut off one internode. This is then pierced by a longitudinal slit and the interior excavated until two notes are produced as on the slit-drum used for drum signalling. This miniature talking drum then serves as a practice instrument for the learner.

Similar accounts of drum language learning are reported for other parts of Africa and for other countries of the world. We are told that in the South Sea Islands:

> . . . very small boys of four and five settle themselves beside small hollow log ends or pieces of bamboo and drum away indefatigably in time with orchestra (of gongs) (23. p. 34).

But Lokele youths and boys are becoming less and less anxious to learn the drum language. Although youngsters can sometimes be heard practising on their pieces of wood in the villages, this is relatively infrequent compared with conditions which must have obtained before the coming of the white man. For the drum language is definitely on the decline. Like many other forms of native art it is suffering from contact with white civilization

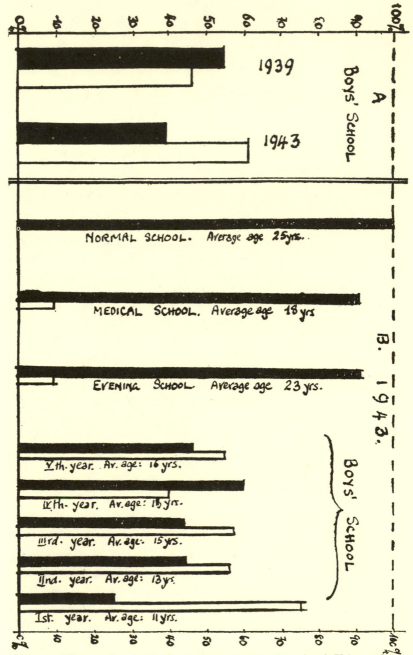

FIG. 12. Diagram showing decline in drum-signalling knowlege in Yakusu schools
A Comparison of % figures for 1939 and 1943   B Analysis of 1943 figures
% knowing drum-language shaded black.   % ignorant of drum language in white

which, partly by offering methods which seem simpler and more advantageous (the possibility of writing letters or of sending messages over enormous distances by wireless, both of which methods of communication can be private whereas the drum is of necessity public in its announcements) and partly by a general disruptive influence on the life of the tribe resultant on the migration of the younger element of the villages to large towns and workers' camps, has led to the eclipse of much of native art all over Africa.

The rapidity with which this decline is taking place can be judged from some statistics obtained in the Yakusu Boys' School. It was first of all agreed that a rough index of the knowledge of drum signalling among the boys could be obtained by assessing their ability to reproduce in full their own drum names, these involving the drum names of their fathers and the names of the towns from which their mothers came (*see* p. 40). The proportion of boys knowing their drum names was first determined in 1939 and then again in 1943, when analyses were made of the numbers of boys with knowledge of the drum language in the various age grades. Results are shown in the accompanying diagram. It is clear that in the short space of four years there is a considerable drop in the number of Yakusu schoolboys who know their drum names; further, this drop is brought about mainly by the entry into the school of smaller, younger boys to whom the drum language means little or nothing. It must not be objected that these boys are too young to have been told their drum names. In traditional Lokele society they would have been given their names and would have learned how to drum them out and to recognize them when drummed long before the age at which boys enter the Yakusu school. The diagram also shows figures obtained in schools for older men and it is seen that almost all of these men know the drum language.

What is thus shown to be true for the drum language of the Lokele people is also true of many another African tribe. Thus for the Ovimbundu of Angola (where signalling was certainly in a code rather than a language) we read:

> drum-signalling has declined with the disappearance of warfare. . . .[1]

[1] HAMBLY, *The Ovimbundu of Angola*, Chicago 1934, p. 334.

and for Dahomey:

> In Dahomey, however, the use of the drum for this purpose would seem to be highly restricted and to be associated almost entirely with drumming the praise-names and messages of monarchs and chiefs . . . whether the absence of drum signalling is to be accounted for by the unwillingness of the monarchy to permit a technique that might easily be put to subversive uses . . . or whether there were other reasons cannot be answered.[1]

All missionaries and Government officers interested in the future of Africa and her peoples know only too well that the rising generation in most parts of the continent shows an eagerness to acquire the new skills of the white man and to jettison without qualms the older arts of former generations of the tribe. Drum signalling is only one example of this new temper. Attempts have been made at Yakusu to foster a respect for the art by arranging definite classes in drum signalling as part of a course in native arts and crafts in the school. This will be continued, it is hoped. But, after some experience of the classes, it is doubtful whether the course will have any real value except for boys who have made the initial steps towards acquiring drumming skill in their own villages. In any case it will be unwise to expect great results from one particular branch of native art until the current attitude of scorn for all things African is removed. It is necessary that as much as possible of present-day knowledge of African drumming in the areas where it is still practised should be set down in records so that, when the interest in African art is awakened among the peoples of the continent there shall be a background of knowledge on which to work. Let us hope that Africans — better equipped in their intimate knowledge of tonal languages and their own customs than the European worker — will interest themselves in these oral literature records so as to increase our knowledge of them. They will be carrying on and appreciating the artistic efforts of former generations of Africans who, to quote Rattray's account of the Ashanti drum language:

> . . . have adapted elements of the science of phonetics to the evolution of a very useful means of inter-communication and

[1] HERSKOVITS, M. J., *Dahomey – an ancient African Kingdom*, New York 1938, pp. 318, 319.

one which is not only of practical utility in their daily life but which has helped to preserve the records of their past, thereby imparting a certain pride of race (30. p. 226 et seq.).

The African of our European High Schools and Colleges studies with zest the records of past generations of Europeans and their culture. Will he accept the challenge of his own past culture, which many of his European friends regard as highly valuable, and give us an account of the Art of Africa in its various forms, many of which seem to be disappearing as white influence increases its scope and power in the country?

And with it the sound of the drum — the everlasting drum.
Stimulus to labour, spirit of the dance,
dirge at the death-bed, call to the feast,
frenzy-lasher at the religious ceremonial
medium of converse
telephone and telegraph in one;
borne across the waters,
booming through the sombre forest,
cheering on the railway cutters —

the fascinating, tedious, mysterious, maddening, attractive, symbolic, inevitable, everlasting, AFRICAN DRUM!

(MOREL, *Nigeria*, London 1912, p. 32.)

THE STORY OF THE TORTOISE AND THE JACKAL

EVERY Central African tribe has a fund of fables about animals and men. The point of some of these stories, however, is unintelligible to the foreigner because the drum language helps in the development of the plot. In the following story the ability of the African to express language on a two-toned whistle is invoked to show how the tortoise is impudent to his enemy, the jackal.

One day the tortoise set out into the forest to venge his wrath on the jackal who had stolen a carcass of fat wild pig which the tortoise had caught in a trap. On his way he came to a garden of banana trees and began to feel hungry. Not being able to climb up the stems he wandered through the garden until he saw a tree in which a monkey was helping himself to the fruit.

'Throw me some fruit down, Monkey,' pleaded the tortoise.

'Climb up here for yourself, Tortoise. Don't you know how to climb?'

'I can climb as well as anyone,' countered the tortoise, 'but I am feeling too tired.'

So the monkey came down and, putting the tortoise on his back, hitched him up among the bananas. The tortoise ate until his hunger was appeased.

But just as the tortoise was casting about for some way of getting down from the banana tree, his enemy the jackal walked into the garden and saw him in the banana tree.

'I am feeling very hungry, Tortoise,' shouted the jackal. 'Please give me some bananas.'

'Come underneath the tree, then,' replied the tortoise. 'Open your mouth and I will throw you some fruit.'

The jackal did as he was told. The tortoise let himself fall out of the tree right on to his enemy and crushed him to death beneath his heavy shell. Then the tortoise cut open the leg of the jackal, took out his thigh-bone and made a whistle of it. He went back to his house whistling merrily:

> The bone of the jackal makes me a flute, fri-fri-fri!
> The bone of the jackal makes me a flute, fri-fri-fri!

As the tortoise whistled away through the forest the brother of the murdered jackal heard the sound and was surprised at the message. He came running up to the tortoise.

'What are you playing on your whistle, Tortoise?' he asked.

'I was playing: "The bone of the antelope makes me a flute, fri-fri-fri!" ' replied the tortoise, nervously.

'But that is not what I heard,' said the brother of the jackal, menacingly.

'It must be because you were too near to me,' lied the tortoise. 'Stay here while I go over by that tree and listen to me again.'

So the tortoise moved over to a tree which had a big hole beneath it; and, standing at the mouth of the hole he played again:

> The bone of the jackal makes me a flute, fri-fri-fri!
> The bone of the jackal makes me a flute, fri-fri-fri!

As the infuriated jackal ran to catch him, the tortoise slipped into the big hole under the tree and the jackal could not reach him.

'I'm going to dig you out, Tortoise,' shouted the jackal down the hole. And he stopped a passing toad and asked him to keep watch at the mouth of the hole while he himself returned to his house to fetch a pick and shovel.

When the jackal had gone away the tortoise came out to the mouth of the hole and said to the toad:

'Can you see me yet, Toad?'

'No, not very clearly, it is too dark.'

'Then open your eyes wider,' counselled the Tortoise.

And as the toad opened his eyes the tortoise threw into them a handful of dirt and escaped quickly out of the hole.

The jackal came back with pick and shovel and dug away at the hole, but he could find no tortoise there. He dug away again and again until he realized that the tortoise had escaped. So he turned on to the poor toad who was watching the digging and killed him.

SIGNS AND SYMBOLS

EXCEPT when quoting from other authors, names and words in Central African languages are written in the symbols recommended by the International Phonetic Association. Approximate equivalents are as follows:

Consonants

b, d, f, g, h, j, k, l, m, n, p, s, t, v, w, and y are as in English.

ɓ or 'b, called *implosive b* is made by sounding the consonant with a slight intake of breath instead of the output of breath as in the English b.

d is made with the tip of the tongue curled up so as to touch the palate instead of the back of the teeth as in English d.

ʃ is the *sh* sound in bu*sh*.

c is used for the *ch* of *church*.

ƒ is an f made with the lips together as if to blow out a candle.

Vowels

a is between the *a* of fl*a*t and that of h*a*rd

e as in French *été*

ɛ as in English w*e*ll or French fen*ê*tre

i is the *ee* of English s*ee*

o as in h*o*pe

ɔ as in h*o*t

u as the *oo* sound of English f*oo*l

Tone signs

It is usual to represent the tonal patterns of words by means of dots placed between square brackets. A dot near the base line of the brackets represents a low-pitched tone while one near the upper line of the brackets represents a high-pitched tone. Mid-tones are then shown by dots in intermediate positions. Gliding tones, when the voice slurs from a low to a high-tone or vice versa, are shown by a curved line:

a [˙] vowel *a* on a high tone; a[.] vowel *a* on a low tone;

a [·], a [.] vowel *a* on two different mid-tones;

a [ )] a glide from low to high; a [\ ] from high to low;

a [,], a [′] glides from low to mid and from mid to high, tones.

Tribal names

The nomenclature of Central African tribes is often complicated by the fact that the name used by a tribe to speak of its
own members is different from the name given to that tribe
by surrounding peoples. So far as possible the names used in
this book are those used by the tribes themselves. Thus:

> the bAngwa are called baNgelema by the Lokele people
> the Mbae are called baManga by the Lokele and other
> tribes

It is usual to prefix ba- to the name of a tribe when referring
to the people of that tribe. The vowel *a* may elide before
other vowels and so we get such names as bOlombo (=ba-
Olombo) and bAngwa (=baAngwa). Sudanic tribes do not
use this prefix, however, and hence it is correct to speak of
the Mbae rather than the baMbae tribe to the north of
Stanleyville.

BIBLIOGRAPHY

THERE are very few, if any books, other than the present, devoted entirely to an account of the talking drums of Africa. The following reading list gives books in which chapters or sections contain an account of the drums (or other instruments) and their language or experiences of the value of the talking drum in native life.

For readers interested in examining the scientific literature on the subject we append a list of papers, most of which give accurate accounts of the relationship between the drummed and spoken languages of Central and West Africa.

General

1. GOODWIN, A. J. H., *Communication has been established*, London 1937. Chap. XIV.

Africa. Congo

2. CRAWFORD, D., *Back to the Long Grass*, London.
3. DENNETT, R. E., *At the Back of the Black Man's Mind*, London 1906.
   N.B. The account of the relationship between language and drumming given here is not sound.
4. JOHNSTON, H. H., *George Grenfell and the Congo*, London 1908.
5. LLOYD, A. B., *In Dwarf Land and Cannibal Country*, London 1899.
6. PIGAFETTA, F., *A Report of the Kingdom of Congo*, Rome 1591, London 1881.
7. ROOME, W. J. W., *Tramping through Africa*, London 1930.
8. SIMPSON, W. H., *Land and Peoples of the Kasai*, London 1911.
9. STANLEY, H. M., *Through the Dark Continent*, vol. II, London. 1878.
10. STANLEY, H. M., *The Founding of the Congo Free State*, London 1885.
11. SUTTON SMITH, *Yakusu the Very Heart of Africa*, London 1910.
12. TORDAY, E., *On the trail of the Bushongo*, London 1925.

BIBLIOGRAPHY

West Africa

13. BASDEN, G. T., *The Niger Ibos*, London 1938.
14. DELANO, I. O., *The Soul of Nigeria*, London 1937.
15. MUNGO PARK, *Travels: 1795, 1796, 1797*, London 1800.
16. PARTRIDGE, C., *Cross River Natives*, London 1905.
17. RATTRAY, R. S., *Ashanti*, Oxford 1923.
18. TALBOT, P. A., *The Peoples of Southern Nigeria*, vol. III, 'Ethnology', London 1926.
19. TROTTER, ALLEN and THOMPSON, *A Narrative of the Expedition sent by Her Majesty's Government to the River Niger in 1841*, London 1848.

South America

20. KARSTEN, R., *The Head-hunters of the Western Amazonas*, Helsingfors 1935.

South Sea Islands

21. BATESON, G., *Naven — A Survey of Problems suggested by a Composite Picture of the Culture of a New Guinea Tribe*, Cambridge 1936.
22. DEACON, A. B., *Malekula — a Vanishing People in the New Hebrides*, London 1934.
23. MEAD, M., *Growing up in New Guinea*, London 1931.

Scientific Papers on the drum-languages of Africa

24. BURSSENS, A., *Le Luba, langue à intonation, et le tambour-signal*. 'Proceedings of the 3rd International Congress of Phonetic Sciences', Ghent 1938, p. 503.
25. CARRINGTON, J. F., *The drum language of the Lokele Tribe*, 'African Studies', vol. 3, No. 2, June 1944.
26. CLARKE, R. T., *The drum language of the Tumba Tribe*, 'American Journal of Sociology', 1934, vol. 40.
27. VAN GOETHEM, L., *Lokole of tam-tam bij de Nkundo-negers*, 'Congo', 1927 II, 1928 I.
28. HULSTAERT, G., *De telefoon der Nkundo (Belgisch Kongo)*, 'Anthropos', 1935, vol. 30.
29. MEINHOF, C., *Die Geheimsprache Afrikas*, 'Globus', 1894, Bd. LXVI.

30. RATTRAY, R. S., *The drum language of West Africa*, 'Journal of the African Society', 1922-23, vol. XXII.

31. THILENIUS, MEINHOF UND HEINETZ, *Die Trommelsprache in Afrika und in der Südsee*, 'Vox', 1916.

32. VERBEKEN, A., *Le tambour-téléphone chez les indigènes de l'Afrique Centrale*, 'Congo', 1920 I, 1924 I.

33. VERBEKEN, A., *La communication à distance chez les noirs*, Elisabethville 1920.

34. WESTERMANN, D., *Zeichensprache des Ewevolkes in Deutsch-Togo*, 'Mitteilungen des Seminars für Orientalische Sprachen', 1907, Bd. X.

35. WITTE, P. A., *Zur Trommelsprache bei der Ewe-Leuten*, 'Anthropos', 1910, Bd. V.

INDEX

INDEX

95

INDEX